BOBBY MOORE
The Master

In aid of

BOBBY MOORE FUND

CANCER RESEARCH UK

NGB

An NGB Publishing publication

© Norman Giller 2013

First published in 2013 by NGB Publishing

10 9 8 7 6 5 4 3 2 1

A CIP catalogue for this title is available from the British Library

ISBN 978-0-9567711-8-6

Typeset and designed by NGB Publishing, Hampshire, UK

Printed and bound by CPI Group (UK) Ltd, Croydon, CR0 4YY

48-50 Birch Close, Eastbourne, East Sussex BN23 6PE

Illustrations © 2013 Art Turner

Photographs from Press Association Images and personal collection

**Special thanks to Ali Cleveland and her colleagues at Cancer Research UK
for their co-operation and encouragement**

BOBBY MOORE
The Master

All profits to the Bobby Moore Cancer Fund

NORMAN GILLER
with an army of eyewitnesses

Introduced by Stephanie Moore MBE

Illustrations: ART TURNER

NGB

Dedicated to the memory of
Bobby Moore OBE
1941-1993

Whether claret and blue
England red or white,
He stood tall and true,
Played with all his might.
He was the Great Defender
Who led with grace and style,
He would never ever surrender;
We remember him with a smile

Bobby Moore, The Master: Contents

Bobby and Stephanie married at Chelsea Register Office on December 4 1991

Introduction: Stephanie Moore MBE

IT seems almost unbelievable that it's twenty years since my husband Bobby died. He'd been suffering from bowel cancer, and to this day his passing causes grief far beyond the football world in which he remains a legend.

Let me say straight away that I am unable to authenticate the football facts and statistics within this book – that is where Norman Giller's great knowledge about Bobby's football career comes into play. I am, however, delighted to give my support to this book in the knowledge that £5.00 for every copy sold on-line will go to the Bobby Moore Fund, the charity I founded in partnership with Cancer Research UK shortly after Bobby died. The Fund also benefits from any copies sold in shops and stores.

An appeal of the book when Norman first outlined it to me is that it focuses on Bobby the footballer, putting into historic context his extraordinary achievements at both club and country level.

In his role as a sportswriter, Norman first interviewed Bobby when he was a sixteen year old West Ham apprentice and followed his career closely from then on, and they became good friends for more than thirty years. For the first time in any book about Bobby, every one of the England teams – which he captained a record-equalling 90 times – is listed along with a match summary and Bobby's memory of the game.

Giving Norman extra motivation for writing this tribute memoir is that he personally has benefitted from the in-depth research into bowel cancer. Norman had a tumour removed from his bowel during a major operation in 2007, and knows that if it had not been for the research of the last 20 years he would not have survived this disease.

My hope is that this book will help raise the awareness of bowel cancer. The cold facts are that 44 men and women die from this disease every day in the UK; it is the UK's second highest killing cancer, yet 9 out of 10 people could be treated successfully if only it were diagnosed early. It is only by raising awareness of the disease and what can be done to combat it, that we can reduce these dreadful figures.

When Bobby was first diagnosed with bowel cancer in 1991 health professionals had great difficulty differentiating between bowel cancer symptoms and irritable bowel symptoms resulting in late identification and often fatal outcomes, as in Bobby's case.

In the last 20 years I have seen massive progress leading to earlier diagnosis, better surgery and treatment.

Initially when I founded the charity in Bobby's memory my objective was to raise £1 million for vital research. I quickly became aware that in terms of research that is a tiny amount, that scientific and clinical research is very expensive and very time consuming, and I realised that I had a responsibility to try to make a difference if we were going to achieve a lasting impact in Bobby's name. By working in partnership with Cancer Research UK I can rest assured that the funds raised are ring fenced for dedicated bowel cancer research in Bobby's name and will be spent on vital exploration of the highest quality.

Our devoted team is small, five young people working at Cancer Research UK headquarters in the Angel area of London, but we have the expert and professional support of a robust and globally respected charity in Cancer Research UK. To date the Bobby Moore Fund has raised more than £18.8 million, and we have ambitious plans for many fund-boosting events that will help the research teams in their never-ending quest to beat bowel cancer. You can find out more about the causes and cures and keep up to date with our plans and projects on line at www.bobbymoorefund.org

There was world-wide mourning when Bobby passed away 20 years ago. We built statues and staged matches in his memory, but what will really make his name live on is to keep battling against bowel cancer until we have it beaten.

This is the story of a great footballer and his wonderful playing career. Hopefully it will also serve as a reminder to you and your loved ones to accept responsibility for your own health and be aware of the symptoms of bowel cancer and make sure that if you have even a hint of them you go and see your doctor early. If you are one of those offered bowel cancer screening, please see that you do it. Remember, the earlier it is caught the better the chances of survival.

Norman Giller, author of this, his 94th book, is living proof that early diagnosis is essential. Enjoy taking the journey with Norman through the footballing life and times of the man I was proud to lovingly call my husband and best friend, the unique, the matchless Bobby Moore. Yes, The Master.

THE purpose of this book is to pay tribute to Bobby Moore, footballer supreme. The Master. If you want the tittle tattle of his life and times, then this is not for you. I am only interested in cementing the facts of Bobby's extraordinary 1,000-match career, concentrating on what he achieved on the playing fields of England rather than recording the peaks and troughs of his private life.

If you want the intimate details of his existence away from the game, then I highly recommend the biography lovingly chiselled by our mutual friend Jeff Powell. My focus will be mostly on Bobby the footballer, and trying to analyse how a player who famously lacked pace and was weak in the air managed to establish himself as one of the greatest defenders ever to step on a football pitch.

It would be arrogant and self-indulgent to try to tell the immense story of his playing career on my own, so I am calling on an army of eyewitnesses to help me. And for the first time in any book, I will be giving a summary and team line-up for every one of Bobby's 108 England matches, along with his observations, which makes this essential reading for anybody interested in the golden age of English football. And Bobby was its golden hero.

I am in a better position than most to accurately account for every one of his England games, because in 1975 I collected and collated quotes from Bobby while organising with my then business partner, Peter Lorenzo, a testimonial dinner for Alf Ramsey at London's Café Royal. We produced a report on every one of Alf's games, 100 of which featured the man he called 'my captain'. All these years later it is rewarding to be able to resurrect Bobby's quotes for such a deserving cause as the Bobby Moore Cancer Fund. I know he would have fully approved.

Our hero passed on all too early in 1993 at the age of 51, the victim of bowel cancer, and I am writing this book in association with the Bobby Moore Fund to mark the 20th anniversary since his widow, Stephanie, started the Fund in partnership with Cancer Research UK. Many people run marathons for the charity. My old legs are not up to that, so I have written this book as my contribution to a deserving cause. A guaranteed £5 for every copy sold on line will be going to the Fund plus a donation from bookshop sales, so hopefully you will not only get a good read but a good feeling for helping such a worthy cause.

Bobby the West Ham apprentice in 1958, aged seventeen

More than £18-million has so far been raised by the Bobby Moore Fund to help finance research into one of the most common and brutal of the cancers, and I am one of those lucky ones who has benefitted from the improved knowledge of recent years. I was diagnosed with bowel cancer in 2007, and thanks to the advancement of medical data – considerably helped by research money – I have (so far) survived following a major operation. The surgeon told me he'd removed a tumour the size of Mike Tyson's fist, and I responded that I was glad it was not as big as another part of his anatomy. I have cleaned that up, but it's no laughing matter and while telling Bobby Moore's inspirational story I hope to raise awareness of why everything must be done to combat the disease that, tragically, beat one of England's greatest sporting icons.

Let me lay out my credentials for being perfectly equipped to tell the story of Bobby Moore the footballer: I was one of the first journalists ever to interview him when I was a reporter (later sports editor) of the local West Ham paper, the *Stratford Express*. Bobby was just sixteen and featured in a 1957 series I wrote called The Apprentice, long before Alan Sugar came on the scene. I was there as a witness as The Apprentice became The Master of Upton Park.

By the time he reached his peak I was chief football writer on the *Daily Express* (in the era when it sold 4.2 million copies a day rather than a week), and I can boast that I was the only newspaperman to get into the England dressing-room following their 1966 World Cup triumph at Wembley. I managed to hug Bobby and touch the Jules Rimet trophy before being ushered out by Alf Ramsey – who even in that moment of euphoria considered the dressing-room private territory .

I was in Mexico at one of the low points of Bobby's life in 1970 after he had been arrested on a trumped-up jewel theft charge, and – following his ordeal – I watched in awe as his masterly performances during the World Cup helped lift him into the land of footballing legend.

He was a notorious insomniac and, as near neighbours in Essex, we used to pass many nights together sharing our mutual love of boxing at the early-morning closed-circuit broadcasts featuring the likes of Muhammad Ali, Sugar Ray Leonard and Tommy Hearns. When I turned up at one of his book launches with Joe Bugner (who I was then representing) Bobby switched the topic of conversation to boxing and astounded everybody by his in-depth knowledge of the Noble Art. He was equally knowledgeable about cricket and in an earlier era would definitely have been an all-rounder in the style of his boyhood hero, Denis Compton.

After matches at West Ham I would be a member of the exclusive Bobby Moore drinking school at watering holes like the Black Lion in Plaistow and the Moby Dick at Chadwell Heath. There were just two rules: you kept your mouth shut about any out-of-school stories you heard and, just as important, you got a round in.

I rarely saw Bobby anything less than immaculate, and I used to jokingly tell him that he had ice rather than blood flowing through his veins. While lesser players would be soaking with perspiration, he would come off the pitch looking as elegant as a David Niven or Cary Grant, and yet his input to the match would have been more productive than any of his team-mates. Actually, he liked to play on the fact that he was more a Steve McQueen clone and looked every inch the hero that he was to a generation of football followers.

Amazingly, Bobby survived testicular cancer two years before he collected the World Cup. I was among a small clique in Fleet Street who hushed up the fact that he'd had a testicle surgically removed. In those uneducated days people kept secret the curse of cancer as if it was almost something of which to be ashamed. Can you imagine the hero he would have become had the nation realised the agony and torture he had been through before his World Cup triumph? Knowing that, perhaps you agree with me that his statue at Wembley should be twice as high.

I watched angrily from the sidelines as the football Establishment snubbed Bobby after he had hung up his boots. This was at the end of a distinguished career, during which he won 108 England caps while captaining his country a record-equalling 90 times; and in three successive seasons he completed an historic hat-trick of collecting the FA Cup, European Cup Winners' Cup and World Cup at Wembley. Those famous 39 steps leading up to the Royal Box were his personal Everest, and he conquered them in 1964, 1965 and then, gloriously, in 1966. Truly a captain marvel.

Bobby shared the record of skippering England most times with Billy Wright, the first player to win 100 England caps and, like Bobby, blond, totally disciplined and immovable in defence. I had the privilege of writing the official biography on Billy – *A Hero for All Seasons* – and both these footballing icons were blessed with the temperament and tenacity that set them apart as born leaders. Sadly, Billy was also cut down by the curse of cancer.

On the personal side, I saw Bobby fall in love twice, first of all with Tina who became his first wife when they were like an early edition of Posh and Becks, with lots of media attention and celebrity trappings. Then, with the early energy going out of his marriage, he confided that he had fallen head over heels with an air hostess he had met in South Africa. This was the beautiful, sophisticated Stephanie, who became his second wife and has ensured his name living on with her drive, determination and dedication on behalf of the Bobby Moore Fund.

But there was somebody who knew Bobby better than even Stephanie and me, and he is my first eyewitness to the footballing life and times of Bobby Moore.

Here comes Greavsie ...

Chapter 1: Mooro and Greavsie

L ONG before Saint and Greavsie there was another double act that was every bit as entertaining and enchanting: Mooro and Greavsie. Who better to call as my first eyewitness of the footballing life and times of Bobby Moore than his best mate in football, the one and only Jimmy Greaves.

They were inseparable on England tours and late in their careers became team-mates at West Ham. Several years earlier, as is revealed in this chapter, they were close to teaming up at Tottenham. Jimmy and I have collaborated on twenty of my 94 books to date, and I spent many happy hours chronicling the movements of Mooro and Greavsie when they were footballing masters on the pitch and drinking partners at the bar. Here's Greavsie on Mooro:

'Every time I think of Bobby, the memories of our experiences and adventures together – off as well as on the pitch – fill me with warm nostalgia. This is then overtaken by feelings of hot anger for the way he was treated after he'd hung up his boots. It was disrespectful, and in my opinion nothing short of disgraceful.

They have erected statues to him at Wembley and at West Ham, named a stand after him, television docos have lauded him, and people who barely knew him have compiled books and websites galore about the master.

To top it all the Football Association – the f****** sweet FA – in 2003 named him their 'Golden Player' of the last 50 years.

Where the f*** were all these fawning people when Bobby was alive? Why couldn't the FA have let him know how precious he was to them before cancer claimed him? They turned their back on him after he had captained his country 90 times in 108 appearances, and played a key role in winning the World Cup for them in 1966. He climbed the 39 steps at the old Wembley for three successive years to collect major trophies, and later had to climb down and almost beg for jobs in the game he had served so well.

Surely it was obvious that the blazered brigade at their then headquarters at Lancaster Gate could have employed him in an ambassadorial role. He was known and

Mooro and Greavsie, the best of mates and both masters of football

admired throughout the world of football, and would have been welcome anywhere as representative of all that was best about our country. Instead of that, when he applied for the England manager's job he didn't even get the courtesy of a reply.

One of the greatest defenders the world has ever seen was forced to scratch a living on the periphery of the game after a few business projects had gone belly-up. He went to Denmark, Hong Kong and those soccer hotspots of Oxford and Southend to earn his bread and butter. He then became 'sports editor' of a daily paper that peddled soft porn before winding up as a pundit-commentator alongside Jonathan Pearce on London radio station Capital Gold, giving his expert opinions on football in between the pop songs.

What a way to treat one of England's finest sportsmen; ignored when alive, acclaimed and applauded in death. It was like reducing Admiral Lord Nelson to the job of looking after the rowing boats at the local park, and then erecting a statue to him. The hypocrisy makes me sick.

I gave a lot of thought to how best I could represent my mate in this book, and decided to dig out an interview my writing partner Norman Giller and I had with him in my early days of switching to media work. Norman knew him as well as I did, and they shared a love of boxing that saw them travelling miles together to catch any fight involving their hero Cassius Clay/Muhammad Ali.

We talked about the good and bad times we had together on and off the pitch. So, if you're sitting comfortably, I shall begin ...

JG: What a jammy git you were, Mooro, to last 90 matches as England captain. I did my best to cost you the job.

BM: There were a couple of times when Alf was on the point of giving me the chop after incidents involving you, James. He went ballistic in New York in 1964 after you'd talked me into breaking a curfew to sneak away from the team hotel to see Ella Fitzgerald singing at Madison Square Garden.

JG: Dear old Alf. When we told him we'd been to see Ella he thought it was an elephant at the circus. All he knew about was football and westerns.

BM: Yeah, he loved his westerns. Remember when we were in East Germany and Alf found out there was a western showing with subtitles? He rounded us up and we all went off to the cinema. The film was dubbed in German, and as the subtitles started crawling along the bottom of the screen they were in Polish!

JG: We pissed ourselves. Alf loved us to do things together, to go round as a team as if tied by a rope.

BM: You were too much of an individualist for him, Jim. Don't forget that we were together on the best day of my life and the worst of yours.

JG: Knew you'd bring that up. We were room sharing in the Hendon Hall hotel during the 1966 World Cup. It was weird when we woke up on on the morning of the final because you *knew* you were going to captain the side and I *guessed* I wouldn't be playing. Alf had not said a dicky bird to me, but I sensed I'd been given the elbow.

BM: What could Alf do, Jim? You'd been injured for the quarter and semi-final and the team had been magnificent in both games. If there had been substitutes then you would have got on, and Geoff probably wouldn't have got his hat-trick.

JG: That's all blood under the bridge, Mooro. I always knew we would win the World Cup but, to be honest, I never envisaged that I'd be a spectator. Remember the first Monday after the opening match of the finals when we went to Pinewood film studios. Sean Connery was making the Bond movie *You Only Live Twice,* and showed us around the set.

BM: I know what's coming. The famous Alf speech. He said, "On behalf of the team, I'd like to thank Seen Connery for his guided tour."

JM: And you said quick as a flash, "That's the funniest thing I've ever shawn or heard." I fell about laughing and Alf was not best pleased with us taking the pee. I wonder if people realise how close you came to not playing in the finals?

BM: Oh, you mean the West Ham contract business. I was virtually blackmailed into signing a new contract with the club just before the first match against Uruguay. Ron Greenwood came to the hotel with all the papers, and it was made clear to me that as I was out of contract with West Ham I would not, under Fifa rules, be eligible to play for England. I'd been hanging out for a hoped-for move to join you at Tottenham, but West Ham kept copping a deaf ear to their approaches. So I put my name to the contract and tied myself to the Hammers. I wasn't being greedy. I just knew I was getting paid half of what many of the players at other clubs were earning.

JG: You'd have loved it at Spurs. Bill Nicholson never made a secret of his admiration for your fooballing talent, and if you'd joined us in those mid-60s I reckon we could have got the League title to go with the FA Cup we won in '67.

BM: Don't rub it in, Jimbo. I was always a fan of that Tottenham team's style of play under Bill Nick. I got several pulls on the old hush-hush including from you that Bill wanted me, but West Ham would not budge. No disrespect to West Ham, but the overall strength of the Spurs squad was far superior back then to what we had at Upton Park.

JG: You were England captain for Alf Ramsey's greatest triumphs, but also for the bad times. There were, for instance, the cock-ups he made with the substitutions in Mexico in 1970.

From the Jimmy Greaves scrapbook: Bobby, in his Steve McQueen lookalike pose, meets "Seen" Connery and Yul Brynner with Greavsie at Pinewood Studios on a rest day during the 1966 World Cup finals

BM: Yes, it was the one weakness with Alf apart from his lack of communication skills with the media. He hated the substitute rule because it had never been part of his thinking in all his time in the game. He never experienced it as a club player or manager, and just didn't feel comfortable with the rule. His decision to pull off Bobby Charlton, who was motoring nicely in the 1970 quarter-final against West Germany, was a shocker. Franz Beckenbauer was standing close to me as Bobby got the hook, and his eyes lit up. He'd suddenly been given hope that Germany could turn the game around.

JG: And you were involved in Kevin Keegan's embarrassing exposure at Wembley.

BM: That was in the 1974 World Cup qualifier against Poland. I'd been dropped after I'd had a bit of a nightmare in the game in Poland. I sat alongside Alf, and had never seen him so lacking in ideas as England struggled to get the ball into the net. I kept on at him in the second-half to get a substitute on to mix things up a bit. But the longer the game went on he just seemed to freeze. Sitting to my right were our subs, including Ray Clemence, Kevin Keegan and Kevin Hector. Suddenly, with just five minutes to go and with me nagging him, Alf finally decided he should send on a sub. 'Kevin, get stripped,' Alf ordered. This was the moment when the drama on the bench turned to farce. Ray Clemence helped Kevin Keegan off with his tracksuit bottoms, but he was so eager that he tugged his shorts down to his knees. While he was suffering this over-exposure he became even further embarrassed when Alf made it clear he meant Kevin Hector not Keegan. I helped Hector off with his tracksuit bottoms, but by the time he got on there were just 100 seconds left – the shortest England debut on record. England went out of the World Cup, and it eventually cost Alf his job.

JG: The most shocked I'd ever known you, Bob, was when I dropped in from nowhere to see you in Mexico City when you were under lock and key in the British ambassador's villa.

BM: That was when I'd been sent back from Colombia after being arrested on that crazy charge of stealing a bracelet from a jeweller's shop on the eve of the 1970 World Cup. Talk about a stitch up.

JG: I'd arrived in Mexico at the end of the World Cup rally to find out that you'd been nicked. Our mutual mate Norman did some detective work and found out where you were being held until allowed to rejoin the England squad. I climbed over the wall of the villa to avoid all the press and photographers at the front, and the ambassador's housekeeper caught me wandering around the garden. She gave me a bollocking and then demanded that I go to the front door. When I rang the door she let me in!

BM: She almost fainted, Jimbo, when your first words to me were, 'Show us the bracelet then, Mooro.' I was so pleased to see you after the nightmare I'd been through. We cleared the ambassador out of all his drink that night.

JG: Once we'd settled down your larger-than-life neighbour from Chigwell, Lou Wade, was allowed to join us, remember? He stood six foot seven and wore a garish check jacket that made him look like a Las Vegas gambler.

BM: The look on the face of the housekeeper when Lou walked in was one of total disbelief. He helped give the ambassador's drinks cabinet a hammering.

JG: It was disgraceful the way Alf and the rest of the Football Association freebie-chasers left you out to dry in Colombia. You could have got thousands out of the jewellery shop for destroying your reputation with a false charge.

BM: I thought of going down that road, Jim, but it would have cost a fortune in legal fees, and knowing what crafty people they were I ran the risk of them inventing some witness who would have pointed the finger at me. Bobby Charlton was in the jewellery shop with me at the time of me supposedly stealing the bracelet. Can you imagine him having anything to do with anything that dodgy!

JG: Or anything dodgy. You could trust him with your last bottle of water in the desert. Remember our dance, Mooro?

BM: You, you silly sod, suddenly grabbed hold of me in the penalty area in the middle of a First Division match between West Ham and Tottenham. You twirled me around as if it was a Cockney knees-up. It was hilarious. Can't imagine that happening in today's game. It's all so bloody serious. As we danced you said, 'See you later at the Black Lion', one of our watering holes.

JG: Happy days. Of course, we wound up together at West Ham.

BM: Yes, and you got me in trouble again. New Year's Day 1971.

JG: Here we go. I'm going to get blamed for the "Blackpool Affair" now.

BM: Well it was you, Jim, who called the cab to take us to Brian London's nightclub when you heard one of the hotel porters say there was no chance of the Cup-tie being played the next day because of all the snow on the pitch.

JG: Let's be honest Mooro, eskimos couldn't have played football in those conditions. And by the way, I didn't call the cab. Two arrived for a TV crew who only needed one. On the spur of the moment we took the spare cab.

BM: I felt sorry for Clyde Best, who we dragged along with us at the last minute.

JG: Yes, Clyde came along for the ride and Stag (Brian Dear) for the drink. We were not pissed when we got back to the Imperial, but we had been seen having a few pints in the nightclub by a supporter. He reported us to the club after we had lost to Blackpool on a skating rink pitch that should have been ruled unfit for play.

BM: It all blew up five days later. Everybody had kept quiet about it because, unbeknown to me, Eamonn Andrews was planning to hit me with the *This Is Your Life* book, and they waited until after the show before the newspapers started headlining what had happened at Blackpool.

JG: I thought Ron Greenwood let you down big time. I didn't care about myself because I was planning to get out of the game at the end of the season. But he just threw you to the wolves. We were both suspended and even Alf Ramsey dropped you for a match. If you'd played it would have meant you beating Billy Wright's record of captaining England 90 times, instead of equalling it. The biggest mistake we made, Mooro, was losing that Cup-tie at Blackpool. If we'd won or got a replay nothing would have come of it. Greenwood could have punished us privately, but decided to let the press have a field day. He used us as scapegoats.

BM: D'you think he was getting his own back for what happened on the plane?

JG: Oh, you mean when that rascal Freddie Harrison spiked his drinks.

BM: We were in the upstairs bar of a Jumbo jet on the way to New York for a friendly match against Pele's Santos. You and I were knocking back pints when Ron joined us and asked for a Coke. Freddie, my business partner, decided to lace the Coke with Bacardi, a pretty juvenile thing to do but we giggled behind Ron's back.

JG: During the next hour or so Ron must have had five or six Cokes, all of them doctored by the mischievous Freddie. Ron finally realised what was going on and, to his credit, he laughed it off. The alcohol made his tongue much looser than he would have liked and he confessed he was thinking of resigning.

BM: Yes, that was embarrassing. And when he went back to his seat he dropped off into a heavy, drink-sedated sleep. Peter Eustace, who was not exactly Ron's greatest fan since being dropped from the team, had the rest of us in fits of laughter as he leant over the snoring Greenwood, miming as if telling him exactly what he thought of him. Ron would have had a fit if he'd woken up.

JG: He never mentioned the resigning business again, but the Blackpool farce certainly gave him the chance to get his own back.

BM: Let's be fair, Jim, for all his faults Ron was a gentleman who gave a lot to the game. He was as good a tactician as I ever met in the game, and he taught me a lot when I was a kid with the England Under-23s and then when he took over from Ted Fenton as manager at Upton Park.

JG: Yeah, Ron was out of the Walter Winterbottom school. A scholar and a gentleman. He couldn't understand how you and I could be less than serious about the game when we were off the pitch. It's history that I hit the bottle, but you could always outdrink me without showing any effect. We used to say you had hollow legs,

BM: I've always enjoyed a good drink, James, as you know. I couldn't believe it when you publicly admitted you were an alcoholic. All of us admire the way you've beaten your problem.

JG: Enough of rabbiting about me. This interview is supposed to be about you. With a gun to your head, who would have been your first choice for a World team from all the players you played with or against?

BM: That's easy, Jim. Pelé by a mile. He had everything – perfect balance, could shoot with either foot, had tremendous vision, was as brave as they come and had the agility of a gymnast. When we appeared together with Sylvester Stallone in the film *Escape to Victory* ...

JG: You were more wooden than the goalposts, Mooro.

BM: Thanks, Jimbo. I didn't expect an Oscar. Anyway, Pele scored with a fantastic bicycle kick. What the public didn't know is that they shot that scene thirty times, and then used the first take! There's no question that Pele was the greatest goalscorer of them all, with you the best of the Brits.

JG: If I was picking a World team defence, Mooro, I'll say this to your face because it's what I say behind your back ... you would be my first choice.

BM: Stop it, Jim. You're making me blush.

JG: Could never understand why you didn't get a shot at a top manager's job. Nobody in the game had a better pedigree than you.

BM: Well I went for the top one, the England post. Sent a a handwritten letter to the FA and didn't even get a reply. Then Elton John gave me the impression I'd got the Watford job and the next I knew he'd given it to Graham Taylor without a dickie bird to me. That disappointed me, Jim. Not so much that I didn't get either job but the way it was handled. Very disrespectful.

I wanted to update the interview for a book we were writing about the greats of the game, and for me there was no greater defender than our Robert. Norman and I had arranged to meet him at the Capital Gold studio in January 1993, but got a call from their switchboard, sending his apologies and asking us to postpone our meeting until a later date.

The interview never took place. Within a month lovely old Mooro had succumbed to his cancer.

One of England's greatest ever footballers – 'Sir' Bobby Moore – had gone, and suddenly everybody cared.

But where were they all when he needed them?**'**

Chapter 2: The Apprentice

IT was the autumn of 1957 when I first met Bobby Moore, and it set me back ninepence to entertain him and his two fellow West Ham apprentices, Andy Smillie and Tony Scott. That was how much it cost for three mugs of tea at Casettari's, a soccer-steeped café opposite the Upton Park ground where the trio of sixteen-year-olds were on the first rung of the professional football ladder.

I was a nervous but enthusiastic young hack of seventeen, taking my first steps on the journalistic path as a reporter on the local *Stratford Express*, which had a circulation of 100,000 and fed off West Ham United as its main source of reader interest and sales.

We were meeting in the foothills of our careers, neither of us realising that within ten years Bobby would be at the Everest peak as World Cup-winning captain, and I would be at the top of my profession as chief football reporter for the *Daily Express*.

I had been given the assignment of interviewing the players for a newspaper series called The Apprentice, long before it became a television vehicle for Alan Sugar.

My brief was to find out the sort of duties young football apprentices had, how much they earned and their ambitions and aims. It was West Ham manager Ted Fenton who suggested Moore, Smillie and Scott as the best representatives of the club and his recently launched youth scheme.

For several seasons West Ham had been losing out to raids on the local schoolboy players by Chelsea, where Stamford Bridge manager Ted Drake was operating his famous 'Drake's Ducklings' youth policy. Among the young protégées stolen from under the noses of West Ham were future England internationals Ken Shellito, Peter Brabrook, Terry Venables and a prolific goal scorer called Jimmy Greaves. All took their first kicks on the playing fields of East London and further east in the football hotbed of Dagenham, and each was poached by an energetic and eccentric Chelsea scout called Jimmy Thompson.

To try to block the Chelsea invasion, Fenton set up a schoolboy scouting network headed by pre-war West Ham player Wally St Pier. He and Fenton were tipped off that there was a defender playing for the Tom Hood Technical High School in Leyton who was worth a look. His name: Robert Frederick Chelsea Moore. Chelsea was a family name and nothing to do with the Stamford Bridge club. St Pier delegated Jack Turner – employed by West Ham as a youth player adviser – to watch him in an Under-15s match at Flanders Road sports ground in East Ham.

Bobby, the quietest and shyest of the three apprentices facing my nervy questioning (it was a toss up whether Bobby or I blushed the most in those days), told me:

‘It was Jack Turner who first approached me after a match, asking if I'd be interested in a career in the game. I'd already made up my mind that I wanted to be either a footballer or a cricketer, and Essex had invited me for trials. But once I knew West Ham wanted me I decided it had to be football. If West Ham hadn't come come in for me I'd probably have studied to become a draughtsman because my best subject at school was technical drawing, but I was sports mad.

I'd have loved to have played football *and* cricket, like my idol Denis Compton, but Jack and then Wally St Pier explained to me that these days you have to choose one or the other.

I'm really enjoying being on the West Ham groundstaff. It's hard work sweeping the terraces, cleaning the toilets, helping do any paintwork or pitch repairs and studding the boots of the first-team players, but it becomes worthwhile when we get to train with the senior squad. I'm being coached by top pros Noel Cantwell and Malcolm Allison, and so I couldn't be in better hands.

My weekly wage is £6.15s (£6-75p), and I get a £3 bonus for playing for the reserves, plus five bob (25p) expenses allowance. My ambition is to get into the West Ham first team and to one day play for England. Both Noel and Malcolm stress the importance of aiming high, and I'm following their advice.’

Within weeks of our interview (certainly one of the first Bobby ever gave), he had made his first appearance for the England youth team under the management of an intelligent and inspiring Arsenal coach called Ron Greenwood. In the years ahead their lives and careers would become inexorably entwined, but not always as cordially as in these early days.

Just a few months after our first meeting Bobby made his League debut for the Hammers, and round about the same time I was promoted to the role of Sports Editor in succession to Harry Miller, an exceptional reporter who went on to giddy heights with the *Daily Mirror* and, later, the *Daily Mail*.

I was right at the heart of all things West Ham, moving from a Cable Street council flat in Stepney to a house in Stratford when I got married at the age of 20 – just ahead of Bobby, who had fallen hopelessly in love with a year younger local beauty called Tina Dean. We all used to ogle Tina when Bobby would arrive at popular Ilford nightspots like Room at the Top and the Palais with her proudly on his arm. Even then they were a glamorous couple who easily took the eye, this before Bobby had started making a name for himself as a local hero footballer.

I was living less than half a mile from what is now the Olympic Park in Stratford, and Bobby and Tina started their married life ten minutes away in a terraced house at Gants Hill. This was three miles from where Bobby had taken his first kicks as a schoolboy in Barking, the suburban town where he was born in Upney Hospital during a Luftwaffe bombing raid on April 12 1941. In those days Barking was in Essex, later becoming part of Greater London. Like neighbouring Dagenham, it was a football-mad area, with the majority of people supporting West Ham.

The Hammers training ground at Chadwell Heath was just a short hop from 43 Waverley Gardens where, when I first met him, Bobby was living with his parents, Poplar-born gas-fitter Bob and his bubbly wife Doris, who had a Salvation Army background. I recall his mother saying: "I never have to clean up after Bobby. He's always neat and tidy." Somehow, that captured Bobby the footballer. None of his team-mates ever had to clean up after him.

He often used to give me a lift from the training ground in what was a flash red Ford Zephyr, and his pride and joy. It was a second-hand car but polished up like new by its proud owner enjoying his first driving adventures. It would be the first of many cars bought by Bobby and – at £375 – by far the cheapest.

The garden of my terraced house in Stratford – more of a yard, actually – backed on to the garden of West Ham goalkeeper Ernie Gregory, who went to on become the Hammers trainer during 50 years service to the club. Round the corner lived chief scout Wally St Pier, one of the most pleasant people in the game. This neighbourliness meant I was never short of inside information about what was going on at West Ham, and both Ernie and Wally were soon enthusing about the young Bobby Moore.

EYEWITNESS WALLY ST PIER

When Bobby first came to our attention we were concerned about his weight. His nickname was Tubby, and it was the extra pounds he was carrying that was the main reason he didn't get top schoolboy representative honours. He was a chubby lad, and manager Ted Fenton was at first reluctant to commit himself to signing him until I convinced him it was only puppy fat. Once he settled to the West Ham training regime the surplus weight he was carrying quickly fell away, and he developed a perfect physique. He is a disciplined, determined and polite young man, and I'm sure he has a great future. He's got an old head on young shoulders, and listens to what he's told. Too many youngsters seem to think they know it all, but Bobby is always anxious to learn from his elders.

Ernie Gregory was in goal for West Ham when Bobby made his First Division debut against Manchester United at the age of 17 on September 8 1958. He was selected ahead of regular left-half Malcolm Allison, who had been taking turns with Noel Cantwell in coaching him along with the rest of the West Ham youth squad, including youngsters Geoff Hurst and Martin Peters. This spare-time coaching was how the players supplemented their £17-a-week wages in the 'soccer slave' era.

The previous season West Ham had won promotion as Second Division champions, and it was well known that it was the players who were deciding the tactics rather than manager Ted Fenton. Great tactical thinkers like Malcolm Allison, Noel Cantwell, Frank O'Farrell, John Bond, Phil Woosnam and Dave Sexton had earned the club the nickname The Academy, talking football non-stop with passion and professionalism. This was the environment in which Bobby was growing up and he could not not get enough of it. I reported on him playing in a 1957 youth match with this West Ham line-up:

Peter Reader; Joe Kirkup, Harry Cripps; Eddie Bovington, Bobby, Geoff Hurst; Derek Woodley, John Cartwright, Mick Beasley, Andy Smillie, Tony Scott.

Interesting that Bobby was playing at centre-half, with Geoff Hurst alongside him as an orthodox left-half. Waiting in the wings were three players I reported on at local schools level: Ronnie Boyce, Martin Peters and Brian Dear. Bobby was making rapid progress, but it still came as a surprise – particularly to Malcolm Allison – when he was called up for his First Division debut at the age of just seventeen.

EYEWITNESS ERNIE GREGORY

It was a shock to everybody when Bobby was picked ahead of Malcolm following our return to the First Division. Big Mal had been a huge influence at the club, but had been struggling since a lung operation that helped him beat tuberculosis. It was obvious that Bobby was going to develop into a class player, but his promotion to the first-team came earlier than any of us expected. His coolness under pressure was already the talk of the club, and he slipped into the No 6 shirt as if it was made for him.

It was not quite as smooth a transition to first-team football as Ernie recalled. In his second League match three days after a memorable 3-2 victory over Manchester

United, Bobby was given the run around by a skilled Scot called Johnny Quigley as the Hammers crumbled to a 4-0 defeat at Nottingham Forest.

EYEWITNESS NOEL CANTWELL

Bobby got a roasting from Quigley but he learned from it and I can't recall anybody else taking him apart in the same way. It made him work even harder on his game, and he spent hours talking to Malcolm and me about how he could improve. We told him to watch the top players and learn from them. He had been modelling himself on the great Duncan Edwards, who tragically died in the 1958 Munich air disaster, and then he switched to watching Johnny Haynes and studying how he dictated matches not only by his passing but also his positioning. Most of all he took heed of what both Malcolm and I always used to stress, 'Ask yourself what you would do if you got the ball NOW!' This meant he was always a thought and a vital yard ahead of the opponents. I was best man at Bobby's wedding and I told his bride, Tina, that she'd better get used to being a football widow because it was obvious the game was going to claim a lot of his time. Very prophetically, I said he would captain England and just a few years later he and I were rival skippers when I led out Ireland and he led out England. He was the best man that day.

The Moore development was put on hold and he only won permanent promotion from the reserves when West Ham sold regular first-team player John Smith to Tottenham in 1960, a move that pleased me for selfish reasons. I have always had an admiration for Spurs and the football they play and Smith was a top-quality player. The shock was that the man keeping Bobby out of the West Ham team failed to make the expected breakthrough into the Spurs side that was the best in the League by a distance, while his understudy Bobby became a star at Upton Park.

Bobby: ❛We couldn't believe it when Smithy agreed to move to Tottenham. They were on the verge of the winning their historic League and Cup double and it was obvious he'd face a huge challenge for first-team football. But for me it was the best possible news, just when I was beginning to think I was going to be stuck in the reserves for years. Once I got back in the team I was determined never again to be a reserve player. That is soul destroying❜

Malcolm Allison, Bobby's hero who lost his place to him at West Ham

At this early stage in his career, Bobby soaked up knowledge like a sponge and it was one of the great ironies of his life that the man he beat to the No 6 shirt was the mentor from whom he learned most, his idol Malcolm Allison. Despite his in-depth knowledge of the tactics and the intricacies of football, Malcolm had never played in the top flight and his dream of appearing in the First Division disappeared when manager Ted Fenton, on the brutally honest advice of his best friend Noel Cantwell, selected the untried and untested Mooro ahead of him.

**EYEWITNESS
MALCOLM
ALLISON**

I was heartbroken for myself but delighted for Bobby. It was a privilege and a pleasure to be in on the ground floor of his career. Most players could beat him in a training sprint, and his heading was weak. But he was a thinking man's footballer and knew exactly where to be for greatest effect. No matter how crowded the penalty area he was always in command and could put in a wicked tackle if necessary. He was never ever a dirty player, but was as solid as a rock and when he tackled it was with determination and a desire to prove himself the master of the situation. He also instinctively knew when NOT to tackle. You never saw him diving in and committing himself. You could count the number of times you saw Bobby on the ground on the fingers of a one-armed bandit. He realised he lacked pace and so worked at having a quicker mind than anybody else. He knew where everybody who mattered was on the pitch before the ball reached him, and knew exactly what he was going to do with it the second it arrived at his feet. I have never known such an inquisitive young footballer. He was forever asking questions and he was always looking to be with the older players and picking their brains. Bobby was not a natural born genius like a George Best or a Jimmy Greaves, but he had an instinct for the game you could not teach and an obsession to improve even when he was established in the England team. A great role model and a smashing companion.

Bobby's club career was off the launching pad. Now he was ready to step up on to the international stage, and helping to show him the way was a new manager at West Ham. Enter Ron Greenwood, arriving as the new boss at the Boleyn at the same time as the maximum wage was kicked out. Bobby was now earning a huge £35 a week!

Chapter 3: Reverend Ron

WHEN Ron Greenwood arrived at Upton Park as manager in 1961 he knew that in Bobby Moore he had a player around whom he could build and mould a team suited to his high ideals and principles. They already had a rapport through Bobby's appearances for the England youth and Under-23 teams that Greenwood coached.

Ron was a self-educated intellectual, out of the same school as his mentor Walter Winterbottom, the England manager since 1946 and the father of English coaching who had Greenwood as his number one disciple. To understand the relationship between Moore and Greenwood, you need to know Ron's background.

Born in Burnley in 1921, Ron spent his early days in a terraced house in the village of Worsthorne close to the outskirts of the Lancashire mill town. In those hungry '20s, the Greenwood children wore clogs with iron bars underneath; shoes were only for Sunday-best wear. I find it difficult to type clogging and Greenwood in the same sentence because physical violence was always alien to Ron's footballing philosophy.

The Depression hit the Greenwood family hard and they moved to Alperton in Middlesex, when Ron's father became a signwriter at Wembley Stadium. Leaving school at fourteen, Ron followed his father as an apprentice signwriter at Wembley, where thirty years later he would have the greatest triumphs of his managerial career. But all the signs for Greenwood were grim at the end of the 'thirties. He had just joined Chelsea after being spotted playing in a local club side when war was declared on September 3 1939. Like so many of his generation, his best playing years were lost to the Second World War.

Following wartime service in the RAF, during which he played club football with Belfast Celtic and Hull City, he returned to Chelsea, who immediately sold him to Bradford Park Avenue for £3,500, while retaining his registration. He was a strong, constructive right-half at Bradford, but later switched to centre-half.

Brentford brought Greenwood back to London where he linked up with a young, jut-jawed player called Jimmy Hill, who was then a forceful wing-half. The half-back line of Harper-Greenwood-Hill was rated one of the best in the League until broken up when Jimmy moved to Fulham and Ron back to Chelsea, where he won a League championship medal as a member of Ted Drake's title-winning squad of 1954-55. He then teamed up again with Jimmy Hill, this time at Fulham.

Both were fanatical coaches, and attended the FA courses where they were deeply

Ron Greenwood, a manager of high principle and ideals

influenced by the thoughts and theories of Walter Winterbottom.

With a thirst for knowledge that had not been nearly satisfied, Ron embarked on a course of self-education. People meeting him later in life were convinced he was a university graduate. The nearest he got was as coach to the Oxford University team. He also coached Walthamstow Avenue and Eastbourne, before being appointed assistant manager to George Swindin at Arsenal in 1957. Winterbottom rated him an outstanding coach, and put him in charge of the England youth team and Under-23s. The player who impressed him most was a young West Ham wing-half called Bobby Moore.

Bobby: ❛I was really excited when I heard that Ron was taking over from Ted Fenton as manager. He had a vast knowledge of the finer points of the game and I was sure we were going to have success under him. I was still learning, and knew I could pick up lots of good tips from Ron. In those early days I followed him around like a puppy and listened and learned. He trusted me with the captaincy, and told me that one of the major reasons he took the job was because he felt he could build the team around me. We got on well during his first few seasons.❜

Greenwood put the emphasis on brain before brawn, and bought Johnny 'Budgie' Byrne from Crystal Palace to add skill and invention to the Hammers attack. A young wing-half called Geoff Hurst was converted to a striker, and an exceptional all-rounder by the name of Martin Peters was gradually introduced to first-team football. The new-style West Ham, carrying the unmistakable stamp of Ron Greenwood, was taking shape, with the commanding Bobby Moore keeping everything tight and tidy at the back.

**EYEWITNESS
GEOFF
HURST**

Ron turned us into thinking footballers, and showed us that the game was as much about using the mind as the feet. The style of play he developed was attractive to watch, though perhaps not suited to the nine-month slog of the League. I owed him so much, because he saw my potential as a goal scorer, while I was struggling to make the breakthrough as a wing-half. Back in those first few seasons Bobby, along with the rest of us, fully respected Ron and we knew he was making us better, more thoughtful players. Few could match his knowledge of world football, and he deserved to get a crack at the England job years before he finally got his chance.

Behind his back, we in the media called Greenwood 'Reverend Ron' because there was something of a preacher about him. He was a committed, church-going Christian, and many of his lectures on football used to come across like sermons from the pulpit. In those early days, Bobby hung on his every word. Greenwood was almost Corinthian in his approach to the game and detested the brutal side of football, so he was appalled when Bobby got sent off for kicking an opponent. This was in a First Division match against Manchester City at Maine Road on November 4 1961, and for one of the few times in his career Bobby completely lost his temper.

> *Bobby:* 'It was the last minute of the match and City had an irritating winger called David Wagstaffe, who had been niggling me throughout the game. I had gone past him to chase a pass from Joe Kirkup when he kicked me from behind, right across the back of my calves. I saw red and turned and kicked him back. He went down as if shot, and the referee sent me off. It taught me a lesson ... never lose your temper on the football pitch. Get your revenge with football skill.'

This was a philosophy Bobby followed for the rest of his playing days, and he was only sent off once more right at the end of his career when with Fulham.

Earlier in 1961 I had earned brownie points by getting Bobby a ringside ticket to watch one of his idols, West Ham 'Golden Boy' Terry Spinks, boxing at Wembley. I rang him the day after his sending-off to say, jokingly, that I hoped the violence had not rubbed off on him. When I delivered the eulogy at Terry's funeral in 2012 I described him and Bobby as being like Golden Boy brothers forged in the same West Ham foundry.

Bobby was given a stern talking to by Greenwood, who told him that if he didn't bring his must-win temperament under control it could cost him a future as an international player. He was already a regular in the England Under-23 team, but in that rollercoaster season of 1961-62 he did not believe he had yet done enough to challenge the likes of Bobby Robson and Stan Anderson for their places in the senior team.

In May 1962 Greenwood called him into his office and told him with a straight face, "I've got bad news for you. You're not coming on our close-season club tour."

Bobby gulped. "What have I done wrong?" he asked, unaccustomed to finding the usually serious Greenwood in a winding-up mood.

"The good news, Walter's been on the phone," Ron revealed. "He wants you for the World Cup squad in Chile."

Bobby's great England adventure was about to start, and it brings us to the main thrust of this book. Threaded throughout the following pages are summary reports of every one of his 108 international appearances, with comments from Bobby and input from team-mates. It captures the golden era of English football, shaken and stirred with the ups and downs of one of the greatest of all playing careers.

CAP 1:
Peru, Lima, 20.5.62. England won 4-0
Springett Armfield Wilson Moore Norman Flowers[1p]
Douglas Greaves[3] Hitchens Haynes* Charlton R.

Highlights: The final warm-up match before the 1962 World Cup finals was notable for a hat-trick from Jimmy Greaves and the cool, commanding debut performance of twenty-one-year-old West Ham wing-half Bobby Moore, who replaced Bobby Robson at right-half. Ron Flowers gave England the lead from the penalty spot before Greaves scored his three goals. Jimmy also put a shot against a post and captain Johnny Haynes hit the crossbar. Ron Springett saved a spot-kick to become the first England goalkeeper to make two penalty saves. Tottenham centre-half Maurice Norman made his bow at the heart of the defence after Peter Swan had pulled out with tonsillitis.

BOBBY: ❛I was astonished to get the call-up and, to be honest, I thought I was going along for the ride just to get the experience. Even when I played against Peru I was convinced it would be just a one-off, with Bobby Robson coming back into the team for the World Cup. Greavsie was outstanding against Peru, and could easily have had half a dozen goals. He was always my favourite English footballer and it was a thrill to play with him. It was one of the big jokes among the players that I went through the entire tour with one of the old FA selectors calling me Ron. He thought I was Ron Flowers.❜

CAP 2
Hungary, World Cup, Rancagua, 31.5.62. England lost 2-1
Springett Armfield Wilson Moore Norman Flowers[1p]
Douglas Greaves Hitchens Haynes* Charlton R.

Highlights: A depressing start to the World Cup. Ron Springett was deceived by the flight of a 15-yard shot from Tichy in the 20th minute, and from then on England were struggling to get into the game on a wet, slippery surface that made every step a challenge. Fifteen minutes into the second-half a goal-bound Greaves shot was handled on the line, and Ron Flowers scored from the penalty spot. Flowers later slipped on the soaked turf and left Florian Albert free to race away and score the winner.

BOBBY: ❛That defeat really hurt, particularly as their first goal was scored by Tichy. I was supposed to be marking him, but the pitch was treacherous because of the rain and it was almost impossible to keep your feet. Ron Flowers went flying as he tried to stop Albert making the break for the winning goal. I wonder if the FA selector thought it was me slipping over?❜

CAP 3
Argentina, World Cup, Rancagua, 2.6.62. England won 3-1
Springett   Armfield   Wilson   Moore   Norman   Flowers[1p]
Douglas   Greaves[1]   Peacock   Haynes*   Charlton R.[1]

Highlights: Alan Peacock, evading the brutal attentions of Argentine captain Ruben Navarro, thought he had started his international career with an early goal when he headed a Charlton cross wide of the goalkeeper. But Navarro managed to push the ball out with his hand. Ice-cool Flowers scored from the spot for the third successive match. Charlton then crashed in one of his specials, and midway through the second half Jimmy Greaves made it 3-0 after the 'keeper had failed to hold a Douglas cross. A defensive muddle let Sanfillipo in for a late consolation goal. Suddenly, the confidence started to return to a team that had been down in the dumps because of 1) their form and 2) a training camp situated in the middle of nowhere that depressed the players.

> *BOBBY*: As the new boy I couldn't say too much, but it was ridiculous the way they tucked us away in a mining area miles from civilisation. Beating Argentina gave us a huge lift, and suddenly the media started to get behind us after dishing out some heavy criticism.

CAP 4
Bulgaria, World Cup, Rancagua, 7.6.62. Drew 0-0
Springett   Armfield   Wilson   Moore   Norman   Flowers
Douglas   Greaves   Peacock   Haynes*   Charlton R.

Highlights: This was without question the most boring, sterile match England had ever contested. They needed only a draw to qualify for the quarter-finals ahead of Argentina, and as Bulgaria showed no inclination to win the match England were content to sit back and make sure they made no mistakes. The result was that the ball hardly left the midfield area and neither goalkeeper was tested. A crowd of barely 6,000 watched the non-event, most of them Argentinians willing the Bulgarians to win, because it would have meant their team progressing through to the quarter-finals. But the Bulgarians did not manage a single serious goal attempt, and England were not much better. It did little to raise hopes for the next match against defending world champions Brazil.

> *BOBBY*: Bulgaria allowed only two players to stray into our half, even for corner kicks! It was the most depressing international in which I ever played. They did not come to play but just to defend. As we only needed a draw we were content to sit back and take no chances. The spectators should have been given their money back.

Johnny Haynes, Bobby's skipper when he made his England debut in 1962

CAP 5
Brazil, World Cup, Vina del Mar, 10.6.62. England lost 3-1

Springett   Armfield   Wilson   Moore   Norman   Flowers
Douglas   Greaves   Hitchens[1]   Haynes*   Charlton R.

Highlights: England's World Cup life was snuffed out by a Brazilian team minus injured Pele but with 'Little Bird' Garrincha at his bewildering best. The ball-conjuring winger put Brazil in the lead 13 minutes before half-time when he headed in a Zagallo corner. England hit back with an equalizer six minutes later, Gerry Hitchens sweeping the ball home after a Jimmy Greaves header had hit the bar. Garrincha decided the match early in the second-half. His powerful free-kick from 25 yards was too hot to handle for Springett, and as he pushed the ball out Vava followed up to head it into the net. Then Garrincha, the man with two left feet, sent a viciously swerving shot curling out of Springett's reach and into the roof of the net.

> *BOBBY*: 'Even without Pele, Brazil were magical. If I hadn't been so busy defending I would have applauded some of their football. Garrincha was just fantastic and almost impossible to mark. He was like Stanley Matthews with a jet engine. It was a privilege to be on the same pitch as a genius.'

Bobby, who had almost automatically become an established England international, returned home from Chile to marry Tina at St Clement's Church in Ilford on June 30 1962. For Tina's side of things you should not miss the revealing biography she wrote in 2006 with the queen of sportswriters, Julie Welch.

There is an hilarious passage where Tina reveals how best man Noel Cantwell and best mate Malcolm Allison followed them out to their honeymoon island of Majorca and got her new husband legless. But the Three Musketeers as they had become were quickly broken up. Big Mal went off to be a professional gambler for a year before starting his eventful coaching career with Bath City, and Noel was sold to Manchester United, where he became skipper and led the Old Trafford team to the FA Cup in 1963. Bobby stayed on to become a fixture at West Ham, never forgetting the vital part Big Mal and Noel had played in laying the foundation to his astonishing career.

He was back under the influence at club level of the deep-thinking Ron Greenwood, who was starting to piece together a Hammers side that was playing some of the most eye-catching football in the League. Bobby and the affable Ken Brown – from the same Bonham Road, Dagenham, district as Terry Venables, the Allen brothers and Boleyn legend Dickie Walker – were as solid a central defensive partnership as there was in the League. They dovetailed together perfectly, Brown an energetic and enthusiastic centre-half and Moore cold, calculating and completely committed to keeping out the opposition.

While Bobby was all style and elegance, I was more of a no-nonsense player and concentrated on getting the ball out of the danger area. Sometimes I would bash it up in the air and Bobby would give me a sidelongs look. I would say, 'Well while it's up there it's not going into our net.' Bobby was an absolute master of positioning and his passing was always thoughtful and positive. It's no secret that he was not the greatest at heading, but I took care of that and won most things in the air. While the rest of us were sometimes dashing around like headless chickens, Bobby would just stroll into position and sort things out with a few barked commands and a perfectly timed tackle. He was a captain who led by example, never bullying but quietly demanding extra effort. There have been few better defenders in the history of the game.

As Greenwood helped bring more discipline into Moore's game, Bobby continued to play on the right side of England's defence even though he now always wore the number six shirt for club matches. He wondered and worried whether he would retain his place after England's mixed performances in the World Cup finals, but Walter Winterbottom continued to have complete faith in him as he prepared to depart from the England manager's job.

CAP 6
France, Hillsborough, 3.10.62. Drew 1-1

Springett Armfield* Wilson Moore Norman Flowers[1]
Hellawell Crowe Charnley Greaves Hinton

Highlights: Walter Winterbottom was working out his notice, Johnny Haynes was recovering from injuries received in a car smash and Bobby Charlton was still not fit after a hernia operation. Mike Hellawell, Chris Crowe, Ray Chamley and skilled Wolves winger Alan Hinton were brought together in an experimental forward line that never looked like clicking in this European championship qualifying match. A Ron Flowers penalty saved England from defeat against a French team skippered by the old fox Raymond Kopa. Maurice Norman was booed every time he touched the ball on the home ground of Peter Swan, the man he had replaced at centre-half.

BOBBY: ❛This was my first full international on an English ground, and I was so disappointed with the atmosphere at Hillsborough. Wednesday hero Peter Swan had lost his place and the fans took their anger out on poor old Maurice Norman, who had taken over from him in the middle of the defence. There was so much chopping and changing among our forwards that we had no rhythm or understanding against a very polished French team in which the veteran master Raymond Kopa was outstanding.❜

CAP 7
Northern Ireland, Windsor Park, 20.10.62. England won 3-1
Springett   Armfield*   Wilson   Moore   Labone   Flowers
Hellawell   Hill F.   Peacock   Greaves[1]   O'Grady[2]

Highlights: Mike O'Grady, twenty-year-old Huddersfield winger and the fifth son of an Irishman, was the latest player tried at outside-left. He must have shaken the skeletons of his ancestors as he sank Northern Ireland with two goals. Jimmy Greaves, another player with deep Irish roots, also scored in a match that featured the debut at centre-half of Brian Labone.

BOBBY: ❛How ironic that a player called O'Grady should help us beat the Irish with two goals. Mike was a quick and clever winger out of the old school, and would have won many more caps but for the fact that Alf Ramsey came along and for a while wiped out wide players. He had to wait six years for his next cap!❜

CAP 8
Wales, Wembley, 22.11.62. England won 4-0
Springett   Armfield*   Shaw G.   Moore   Labone   Flowers
Connelly[1]   Hill F.   Peacock[2]   Greaves[1]   Tambling

Highlights: Walter Winterbottom's final match. Alf Ramsey watched from the stand in readiness to take over. There was a crowd of only 27,500 – the lowest to date for a Wembley international – to see England romp to a comfortable victory. Chelsea striker Bobby Tambling made his debut in the No. 11 shirt. Alan Peacock scored two goals, John Connelly one and Greaves netted the last goal of Winterbottom's reign. In the dressing-room after the match skipper Jimmy Armfield presented Walter with a set of crystal cut-glass goblets on behalf of the players. The toast was 'Walter Winterbottom, master manager.' He might have done even better had the amateur selectors left him alone to manage without interference.

During his sixteen years in charge, Winterbottom's record was:

P129 W78 D33 L28 F383 A196.

The fifteen most-capped players during his reign were Billy Wright (105), Tom Finney (76), Johnny Haynes (56), Jimmy Dickinson (48), Bobby Charlton (39), Ron Flowers (39), Stanley Matthews (36), Ronnie Clayton (35), Roger Byrne (33), Bryan Douglas (33), Nat Lofthouse (33), Alf Ramsey (32), Jimmy Armfield (32), Ron Springett (28), Neil Franklin (27).

Franklin would have doubled his caps collection but for dropping out in 1950 to play in the outlawed Colombian league. He was desperately missed by Winterbottom during the disastrous 1950 World Cup campaign. What heights might England have scaled in the 1958 finals but for the Munich air disaster that robbed the team of Roger Byrne, Tommy Taylor and the irreplaceable Duncan Edwards? Winterbottom was not the luckiest of managers.

BOBBY: ❝I found Walter a thorough gentleman, and a walking encyclopaedia on international football. He was the obvious choice to be the new secretary of the Football Association but the job went to the civil servant Denis Follows. Walter walked away from football and became the highly successful head of the Central Sports Council and was quite rightly knighted. I wonder what he would have achieved with England if he had been allowed to select the teams? He was always at the beck and call of amateur selectors, but Alf made it clear he would not stand for that. He was going to be the sole boss.❞

Bobby never forgot his roots and was always accessible to the local press, unlike today when players hide themselves behind security gates and release stilted statements through their agents. He was particularly close to the 'Two Trevors', well-informed *Ilford Recorder* reporter Trevor Smith and the affable Trevor Bond, who had succeeded me as Sports Editor of the *Stratford Express* and later became a powerhouse with the *Sunday Telegraph* and *Mail on Sunday*.

When Bobby returned from his World Cup adventure in Chile he told Bond in an exclusive interview: "I am convinced England, with home advantage, can win the World Cup in 1966."

This was long before he was appointed captain, and before the Football Association failed to persuade Burnley's Jimmy Adamson to take over as England manager. They turned instead to the man who had been born in the same corner of Essex as Bobby. Enter Alf Ramsey.

# Chapter 4: The Ramsey Factor

THE distance between Bobby's birthplace at Upney to a smallholding where Alf Ramsey was born 21 years earlier is just 2.8 miles, or seven minutes in a Ford Zephyr, 25 minutes by horse-drawn caravan. But they were hundreds of miles apart in personality and pastimes. For Alf, football was the be-all-and-end-all, while Bobby liked to enjoy life away from the disciplines of the game. He could drink with the best of them, and we used to say he would captain an England drinking XI. I have rarely known any sportsman match his capacity for sinking lagers, but he was never a lager lout. The more he drank the more docile he became, and this was the only time that his defences would come down; otherwise, Bobby allowed as few people to get close to him as the extremely self-protective Ramsey.

As with Ron Greenwood, Bobby had a footballing rapport with Ramsey, but away from the game they had little in common and they rarely mixed.

While Bobby's Dad was a gas fitter, Alf's father once lived in a caravan, traded in hay and straw and was from gypsy stock. Alf first started learning ball control in what were then the fields of Dagenham with his three brothers Albert, Len and Cyril. These open spaces were soon turned into sprawling housing estates for the overspill population from London's East End, by which time Alf had started his playing career down on the south coast, first as an amateur with Portsmouth and then after wartime army service as an £8-a-week professional with Southampton.

He had the strong, dark looks associated with gypsies, and his non-PC nickname in his early playing days was 'Darkie' Ramsey. But nobody found out for sure about the Ramsey roots because he was always so secretive and sensitive about his background. Once, in a radio interview, he was asked: "Are your parents still alive, Mr Ramsey?" "Oh yes," he replied. "And where do they live?" the interviewer inquired. "In Dagenham, *I believe*," Alf said, leaving listeners and the interviewer puzzled and perplexed.

Alf was determined to keep his private life private, and when a journalist started to write an unofficial biography he asked, in vain, how he could stop its publication. The only 'dirt' the book could dig up was that he had apparently told a porky about his age before signing as a professional with Southampton in 1946, knocking off a couple of years from his birth date of January 22 1920. It was hardly a crime. Sportsmen can be as sensitive as actresses (and authors) when it comes to admitting their age. The book also 'revealed' what all of us close to the village world of football knew – that Ramsey

Sir Alf presents Bobby with the 1966 Daily Express *Sportsman of the Year trophy*

had taken elocution lessons to try to iron out his broad Cockney accent. Alf should have asked for his money back, because the accent he finished up with was so forced that he left himself open to ridicule. He often put aitches in the wrong places and sounded like Dick van Dyke's cardboard Cockney in *Mary Poppins*. But regardless of how he talked he got through to the players because he could speak their language. For all his airs and graces, he was a football man through and through.

He quickly made up for lost time after the war had delayed his entry into the Football League. His studious rather than spectacular play earned him 32 caps as England's reliable right-back, and he brought style and panache to the Tottenham push-and-run team that won the League title in 1950-51 with some of the most elegant football ever witnessed on an English playing field. Eddie Baily was the chief orchestrator:

**EYEWITNESS
EDDIE
BAILY**

We used to call Alf The General. The minute you sat down at a meal table he would have the cruet, the sauce bottle and the sugar bowl on the move as he outlined new tactical ideas. He was also worth listening to about greyhound racing. He knew the form of all the dogs, and was one of the lads when we used to go and cheer on the greyhounds we'd backed at Walthamstow Stadium. It was obvious he was going to become a top manager, but I could never understand why he suddenly got a plum in his mouth. He just didn't seem like the old Alf once he stopped playing and began talking all posh.

Alf became manager of backwoods Third Division South team Ipswich Town, where he came under the influence of the Old Etonian Cobbold brothers. He steered Ipswich into the Second Division in 1956-57, and then in successive seasons in 1960-61 and 1961-62 captured the Second and First Division titles, a repeat of the back-to-back double he enjoyed as a player with Spurs. The remarkable thing was that he did it all on a shoestring budget. The most he ever paid for a player was £12,500, and he conquered the giant money-no-object clubs in the League by brilliant tactical planning.

It was at Ipswich he began to experiment with the revolutionary 4-3-3 formation that was to wing him to lasting fame in the World Cup. Waiting to join him on his glorious adventure was a young blond boy from Barking, Bobby Moore.

CAP 9
France, Paris, 27.2.63. England lost 5-2

Springett Armfield* Henry Moore Labone Flowers
Connelly Tambling[1] Smith[1] Greaves Charlton R.

Highlights: Alf Ramsey's first match – a European championship qualifier – was a personal nightmare for goalkeeper Ron Springett. He was responsible for three of the French goals, his most costly error coming after England had pulled back from 3-0 to 3-2 with goals from Bobby Tambling and the recalled Bobby Smith. Springett, a man of character and charm, did not try to make any excuses, but Ramsey pointed out that he had been kicked in the ribs when conceding the first goal. He was also troubled by the floodlights in the Parc des Princes stadium. Ron Henry, Tottenham's skilful left-back, had an uncomfortable night against flying French winger Wisnieski in his one and only England appearance. Interestingly, just two of the team – Bobby Moore and Bobby Charlton – would survive to play a part in the 1966 World Cup final. Ron Springett was second string goalkeeper in the '66 squad, and was later involved in a unique swap deal with his goalkeeping brother Peter, Ron going to Sheffield Wednesday, with Peter going in exchange to QPR.

BOBBY: ❛Alf seemed cold to people outside the game and even to some inside it, but he was very warm with the players. He had an amazing grasp of football tactics, and a photographic memory when it came to recalling any player he had ever seen. He put his ideas across simply and without the sort of lecturing we often got from Walter and Ron. He took that opening defeat in his stride and knew the scoreline flattered France. Ron Springett, a lovely bloke, had one of those games you would not wish on your worst enemy, and all we players in the squad felt sorry for him.❜

CAP 10
Scotland, Wembley, 6.4.63. England lost 2-1

Banks Armfield* Byrne G. Moore Norman Flowers
Douglas[1] Greaves Smith Melia Charlton R.

Highlights: Both teams were down to ten men within five minutes following a collision between Bobby Smith and Scottish skipper Eric Caldow, who was carried off with a triple fracture of the leg. By the time Smith limped back on with his bruised knee bandaged 'Slim' Jim Baxter had twice beaten England's new goalkeeper Gordon Banks, first after a misplaced pass by Armfield and then from the penalty spot. Bryan Douglas scored ten minutes from the end, but the Scots deserved a victory that was masterminded by Baxter, who memorably walked off with the match ball tucked up inside his jersey. This stunningly skilled showman had owned the pitch, so why not the ball? Liverpool team-mates Gerry Byrne and Jimmy Melia made their debuts. It was the first match played at the 'new' Wembley with a £500,000 roof that ran right round the stadium like a giant lip. A 98,000 crowd paid then record receipts of £76,000. Ramsey had kicked off with two defeats. The topic in the Press Box was. 'Could this be the man to lead England to the World Cup?'

> *BOBBY*: ❛Alf was in a black mood after this match. He hated losing to the Scots more than any other team, and he felt we had allowed Jim Baxter too much space. But that was a day when Slim Jim was just untouchable. Few players in the world could match his passing skill when he was in the right mood. There were rumblings in the newspapers that perhaps Alf was not up to the job, but we players knew we were in good, safe hands.❜

CAP 11
Brazil, Wembley, 8.5.63. Drew 1-1
Banks Armfield* Wilson Milne Norman   Moore
Douglas[1] Greaves Smith Eastham Charlton R.

Highlights: There was no Pele, but Pepe popped up with a first-half 'banana' free-kick from 25 yards that deceived Gordon Banks and swung into the roof of the England net. Douglas scrambled a late equalizer against the world champions. Gordon Milne was the first defensive 'ball winning' midfield player selected by Ramsey, a role that would ultimately go to Nobby Stiles. George Eastham followed his father, George senior, as an England international, and they were the first father and son to win England caps. Gordon Banks said later, 'Alf gave me a rollocking at half-time for falling for what he called Pepe's three-card trick. But from Alf's position on the touchline he could not have known how much bend Pepe put on the ball. I swear that if it had not gone into the net it would have done a circular tour of the stadium!'

> *BOBBY*: ❛This was my first match wearing my favourite No 6 shirt. I don't think I'd ever seen Alf as angry as he was over Gordon letting in that free-kick from Pepe. He kept saying like a stuck record, 'I told you what he'd do with a free-kick ... I told you.' But in fairness to Banksie, the ball went on a crazy swerve and I doubt if any goalkeeper in the world could have stopped it. All in all we were pleased with our performance against the world champions, but Alf was still waiting for his first victory.❜

Chapter 5: Captain of England

BOBBY's captaincy of England started by accident rather than design. Regular skipper Jimmy Armfield was injured and missed the opening match of England's summer tour of Eastern Europe during which Alf wanted to build a team spirit that would carry them all the way through to the 1966 World Cup finals, for which England had automatically qualified as host country.

It was clear that Alf saw Bobby as a natural leader when he named him captain in Armfield's absence, even though his squad was packed with older players with much more international experience than the West Ham skipper. Alf took Bobby on one side during a training session when he heard that the church-going, organ-playing Armfield was not fit enough to play.

"I'd like you to be my captain against Czechoslovakia," he said. "I will understand if you prefer not to at such late notice. I've captained England and know it can be an ordeal." Alf was testing his resolve and ambition.

Bobby later told me that he felt himself almost bursting with pride. "I'd be honoured," he said to Alf. "I know it's just a short-term thing, but for me it's a dream come true."

**EYEWITNESS
GORDON
BANKS**

It was obvious to all of us in the squad that Bobby was the England captain in waiting, and so it was no surprise when Alf named him to lead us out against Czechoslovakia. He always had a bearing about him that made him a natural leader. He led by example and was never a fist-brandishing skipper, but showed us the way by his personal performances. It gave us great confidence to walk out behind him, and he had a bit of that London swagger about him that made you feel good. Bobby was Mr Cool and never let anything get to him. I played with him more than seventy times and can hardly remember seeing him looking ruffled or anything less than composed. It was a pleasure to play with him and count him as a team-mate and pal.

A proud and peerless England captain ... and here, unusually muddy!

CAP 12
Czechoslovakia, Bratislava, 20.5.63. England won 4-2
Banks   Shellito   Wilson   Milne Norman Moore*
Paine   Greaves[2]   Smith[1] Eastham   Charlton R.[1]

Highlights: The first victory under the Ramsey baton, and what an impressive scalp. Czechoslovakia had been runners-up in the 1962 World Cup final and included European footballer of the year Josef Masopust in their midfield. Greaves (2), Smith and Charlton scored the goals, and Ken Shellito and Terry Paine made impressive debuts. A knee injury would virtually end Shellito's career within the year. He was a beautifully balanced player who could match the speed of sprinting wingers. His early retirement would be a blow to Chelsea and England, but George Cohen was - so to speak - waiting in the wings to make the No 2 shirt his personal property. Bobby Moore captained England for the first time in place of the injured Armfield. He would go on to skipper England 90 times, equalling the record set by one of his boyhood heroes Billy Wright (who had been his manager at England Under-23 level).

> *BOBBY*: ❛I had idolised Billy Wright and then Johnny Haynes, and wanted to meet the high standards they had set as England captain. As I walked out at the head of the team I had never been so proud and knew it was a job I wanted full time. The Czechs were going to win that match over my dead body. There is no greater honour than leading your country.❜

CAP 13
East Germany, Leipzig, 2.6.63. England won 2-1
Banks Armfield* Wilson Milne Norman Moore
Paine   Hunt[1] Smith   Eastham   Charlton R.[1]

Highlights: Roger Hunt, playing in place of tonsillitis-victim Greaves, scored a spectacular equalizer from thirty yards after Banks had conceded a soft goal midway through the first-half. Bobby Charlton netted the second-half winner after a series of goalmouth misses against an outpowered East German team.

> *BOBBY*: ❛An England victory in Germany would have had most managers singing their own praises, but Alf proved he was a perfectionist expecting the highest standards when he told us in the dressing-room afterwards: 'Our passing was erratic and careless and lacking in imagination. We can, and will, do much much better.' That was exactly what I wanted to hear. Alf was a winner and was not prepared to settle for second best. ❜

CAP 14
Switzerland, Basle, 5.6.63. England won 8-1
Springett Armfield* Wilson Kay[1] Moore Flowers
Douglas[1] Greaves Byrne J.[2] Melia[1] Charlton R.[3]

Highlights: A hat-trick from Bobby Charlton and two goals from Johnny Byrne helped England bury the Swiss under an avalanche of goals. Everton midfield dynamo Tony Kay scored in his only international appearance before the careers of both he and his former Sheffield Wednesday team-mate Peter Swan were wrecked by a bribery scandal. The sporting Swiss fans gave England a standing ovation at the end, and even poker-faced Alf Ramsey struggled to keep a smile off his face as he said, 'That was much more like it. We played with the urgency and purpose that was missing from the performance in Leipzig. All in all, this has been a most satisfactory summer tour. But there is much work still to be done.' The only surprise was that goal thief Greaves – at the peak of his powers, and six times the leading First Division marksman – failed to get on the scoresheet. But he played an assist role in four of the goals.

BOBBY: ❛We came away from that first tour under Alf feeling quite a buzz. There was a great team spirit on and off the pitch, and you could sense that something special was not far off. This was the match in which Bobby Charlton became joint top England scorer with Tom Finney and Nat Lofthouse, and Alf – who played with both Tom and Nat – led the applause in the dressing-room afterwards. It was great to be part of it.❜

CAP 15
Wales, Ninian Park, 12.10.63. England won 4-0
Banks Armfield* Wilson Milne Norman Moore
Paine Greaves[1] Smith[2] Eastham Charlton R.[1]

Highlights: The double act of Greaves and Smith was unstoppable. Greaves made a goal in the fifth minute for Smith who then returned the compliment before the irrepressible Greaves laid on a second goal for his beefy Tottenham team-mate. Bobby Charlton finished off the Welsh with his thirty-first goal for England, beating the record that he had held jointly with Nat Lofthouse and Tom Finney. 'Preston Plumber' Finney was a guest spectator, and said: 'Bobby will go on to score many more goals for England. The record could not be held by a better player nor a nicer man. He is a credit to the game.' One true gentleman recognizing another. Bobby Charlton wore the number 11 shirt, but followed Ramsey's orders and was more withdrawn than usual ... a sign of things to come.

BOBBY: ❛We were all thrilled for Bobby. I know it was very special for him to have Tom Finney there to see him take over as top scorer for England. Like all of us, we were in awe of Tom, who had been such a wonderful servant for Preston and England. He and Stanley Matthews were huge heroes for all we England players when we were schoolkids just starting to fall in love with the Beautiful Game.❜

CAP 16
Rest of World, Wembley, 23.10.63. England won 2-1
Banks Armfield* Wilson Milne Norman Moore
Paine[1] Greaves[1] Smith Eastham Charlton R.
Rest of the World: Yashin Santos D Schnellinger Pluskal Popluhar Masopust
Kopa Law[1] Di Stefano Eusebio Gento (Subs: Soskic, Eyzaguirre, Baxter, Seeler, Puskas)

Highlights: Jinking Jimmy Greaves was the star turn on the Wembley stage in this prestige match to celebrate the Centenary of the Football Association. He might have had a first-half hat-trick but for the magnificent goalkeeping of Russia's 'Man in Black' Lev Yashin. Terry Paine gave England a first-half lead, which was cancelled out by Denis Law, and it was Greavsie who conjured the winner with just three minutes left of a memorable match. There was a wonderful moment in the first-half that captured the spirit in which the game was played. Yashin had been giving an amazing exhibition of shot stopping, and on the half hour artful dodger Greaves tried for a sixth time to beat him. He fired in a power drive that most goalkeepers would have tried to either tuck away around a post or over the bar. But the unpredictable Russian met it with a boxer's punch that sent the ball screaming back to the halfway line. Greaves and Yashin then fell into each other's arms laughing as they congratulated each other. Greavsie then at last got the better of Yashin with what he has since described as the 'greatest goal I never scored!' He threaded his way past four of the world's finest defenders before slipping the ball wide of the oncoming Yashin, but it was disallowed because the referee had – unheard by most people in the stadium - whistled for a foul against Greaves at the start of his scintillating run. What ever happened to the advantage rule, ref?

BOBBY: ❛What a dream of a match against the greatest players in the world. It was wonderful for the British game that the two best forwards on the pitch were Greavsie and – for the Rest of the World – Denis Law. Jimmy in particular was in devastating form, and only the fantasic goalkeeping of Lev Yashin stopped him getting at least a hat-trick. It was like a Who's Who of football. I was the only one I'd never heard of.❜

CAP 17
Northern Ireland, Wembley, 20.11.63. England won 8-3
Banks Armfield* Thomson   Milne   Norman Moore
Paine[3] Greaves[4]   Smith[1] Eastham Charlton R.

Highlights: Greaves (4) and Terry Paine (3) lit up this first match under the Wembley floodlights, and Bobby Smith scored once in what was to be his final international appearance. Smith (12) and Greaves (19) between them collected thirty-one goals in just thirteen matches together. Wolves left-back Bobby Thomson made a sound debut at the age of nineteen. It was England's sixth win in succession under Ramsey, and a mood of optimism was beginning to build with the World Cup finals bound for the birthplace of the game in 1966.

> *BOBBY*: ❝Greavsie was outstanding again. Goalkeeper Harry Gregg, a Munich survivor, playfully grabbed hold of Jimmy at the end and pretended to throttle him. Jim told him, 'Careful, Harry, you might shake my Irish ancestors. My gran's name was Katie O'Riley.' Thank goodness he didn't play for Ireland!❞

CAP 18
Scotland, Hampden Park, 11.4.64. England lost 1-0
Banks Armfield* Wilson Milne Norman Moore
Paine   Hunt   Byrne J. Eastham Charlton R.

Highlights: Roger Hunt and Johnny Byrne deputized for injured Greaves and Smith on a wet and stormy afternoon at Hampden. Alan Gilzean, who was to take over from Smith as partner to Greaves at Spurs, scored the only goal of the match after Gordon Banks had misjudged a seventy-second minute corner-kick from Davie Wilson that got held up in the near-gale force wind. A crowd of 133,245 witnessed a third Scottish victory in a row over the Auld Enemy, the first time this had happened for eighty years.

> *BOBBY*: ❝It was like playing in a wind tunnel, and it was almost impossible to control the ball. Their goal was a real freak effort. Gordon came for Davie Wilson's cross and stretched out to catch it when it just stopped dead and he was left with a handful of nothing. Alan Gilzean sneaked in and scored with one of his trademark flick headers. Nobody could blame Gordon. It was just one of those things.❞

Bobby's calculating mind was now switched to the most momentous club match of his career to date: the FA Cup final at Wembley.

Chapter 6: Footballer of the Year

THE establishment of Bobby at the heart of the England defence coincided with West Ham hitting a golden spell under the influence of Ron Greenwood. They reached the FA Cup final in 1964, and waiting for them at Wembley were Second Division Preston. Two days before the final Bobby was guest of honour of the Football Writers' Association at the Café Royal where he received the supreme accolade of the Footballer of the Year award.

But years later when I interviewed Bobby for a book I was planning with the freelance maestro Dennis Signy on the history of the FWA trophy – *The Golden Heroes* – it was not the FA Cup final that stood tallest in his memory.

BOBBY: ❛It is another match that stands out above all others from that 1963-64 season. West Ham were drawn to face Manchester United in the FA Cup semi-final at Hillsborough. We were supposed to play just a walk-on part against Cup-holders United, who had the likes of Bobby Charlton, Denis Law and a young Irishman called George Best in their team. It was an atrocious afternoon, with non-stop rain turning the pitch into a quagmire. We managed to produce the greatest form of our lives, and won 3-1 to book a place in the final. A few weeks later I was named Footballer of the Year, and I had to go and collect the award on my own 48 hours before the final because of a curfew set by Ron Greenwood. Surely the club could have spared one representative to go with me? I made the point it was as much a reward for the team as for me.

The final against Preston, including seventeen-year-old Howard Kendall, was a big anti-climax. We failed to play anything like our best, and we struggled to win 3-2. I have to admit we were a little fortunate to clinch victory with a late headed goal by that great West Ham loyalist Ronnie 'Ticker' Boyce. What a pity the game against Manchester United was not the final. People would then have seen us produce the sort of storming form that made us the talk of football in those mid-sixties.❜

For the record, West Ham's winning team in that 1964 FA Cup final:

Standen, Bond, Burkett, Bovington, Brown, Moore

Brabrook, Boyce [1], Bryne, Hurst [1], Sissons [1]

**EYEWITNESS
RONNIE
BOYCE**

I had only netted six goals in the League that season, and Ron Greenwood kept encouraging me to come through from midfield to get into scoring positions. It was like a dream come true to score the winning goal in a Wembley cup final. I think I would have run all the way out of the stadium if my team-mates hadn't caught up with me! It was an honour for me to play so many of my games with Bobby Moore as my captain, without question the greatest defender of them all. His composure and commanding presence was astonishing, and he was a great role model for all the young players coming into the game.

Four days after collecting the FA Cup, Bobby was back at Wembley leading out England against Uruguay and now officially the captain, not just a stand-in.

CAP 19
Uruguay, Wembley, 6.5.64. England won 2-1
Banks Cohen Wilson Milne Norman Moore*
Paine Greaves Byrne J.^{2} Eastham Charlton R.

Highlights: George Cohen came in at right-back for the injured Jimmy Armfield, and partnered Ray Wilson for the first time. Ramsey's 1966 World Cup defence was taking shape. Johnny Byrne scored both England goals in an uninspiring match. A week earlier the Uruguayans had been involved in a brawl of a match with Northern Ireland in Belfast, and Alf Ramsey warned his players that on no account should they be drawn into any feuds. The result was a tame game decided by the decisive finishing of Byrne, nicknamed 'Budgie' because he was a non-stop talker both on and off the pitch. He continually had the Uruguayan defence stretched with his precise passing and intelligent positioning.

BOBBY: ❛Some of the Uruguayan tackles were so high that it's a wonder they didn't get snow on their boots. We kept our discipline and it was the skill of my dear old mate Budgie Byrne that won the game for us. He was one of the most creative forwards in the League, and he had the Uruguayan defenders in tangles with his clever play and decisive finishing.❜

For the one and only time, the FA Cup travels by tube. Holding it like a beloved baby is manager Ron Greenwood, and sitting next to him is author Norman Giller, who was then on the Daily Herald. He explains: "King photographer Monte Fresco and I were giving Ron a lift to Soho for a press conference on the Monday after West Ham had won the Cup. We got caught in heavy traffic at Mile End, parked our car and decided to do the rest of the journey by tube. Monte couldn't resist banging off a picture."

CAP 20
Portugal, Lisbon, 17.5.64. England won 4-3
Banks Cohen Wilson Milne Norman Moore*
Thompson Greaves Byrne J.[3] Eastham Charlton R.[1]

Highlights: Johnny Byrne completed a memorable hat-trick in the final moments with a beautifully disguised chip shot from the edge of the penalty area that went over the heads of three defenders and the goalkeeper and into the net. Portugal, who had led twice through the towering Torres – a 6ft 7in centre-forward – and his Benfica side-kick Eusebio, could not believe it. Liverpool dribbler Peter Thompson won his first of sixteen caps as he tried to prove to Ramsey that wingers were a necessary evil. The match was staged to mark the golden anniversary of the Portuguese Football Association, and it was 17 years after England's 10-0 victory in the same picturesque setting of Portugal's National Stadium.

BOBBY: ❝We had a bit of a fall-out with Alf before the game when seven of us went for a late-night bevvy in London's West End, and broke a curfew. When we returned to our rooms we found our passports on our beds. That was Alf's sign that our absence has been spotted. The next day after a training session in Lisbon he told us quietly that he would not tolerate such indiscipline and that any repeat and we would be out of the squad. He picked us all against Portugal, and Budgie Byrne – one of our drinking party – played the game of his life. He won the match for us against an exceptional Portuguese team with a brilliant late goal to complete his hat-trick.❞

CAP 21
Republic of Ireland, Dublin, 24.5.64. England won 3-1
Waiters Cohen Wilson Milne Flowers   Moore*
Thompson Greaves[1] Byrne J.[1] Eastham[1]   Charlton R.

Highlights: Goals from George Eastham and Johnny Byrne gave England a 2-1 half-time lead and Jimmy Greaves wrapped it up in the fifty-fifth minute when he put the finishing touch to a classic five-man move down the right wing involving Milne, Thompson, Byrne and Eastham. Manchester United skipper Noel Cantwell switched from left-back to the middle of the Irish defence in a bid to control Byrne, who was at his brilliant best as he tormented his markers with subtle touches and clever changes of pace. It was not lost on the spectators jammed into Dalymount Park in Dublin that their defence was being tormented by a player with strong Irish ancestry. Tony Waiters, a lifeguard on the Blackpool beach when he was not guarding the Blackpool goal, played the first of his five England games at the back of the England defence.

BOBBY: ❝My good mate Noel Cantwell, best man at my wedding, was my rival captain and he came off the pitch at the end with a sunburned tongue after Budgie Byrne had given him a good chasing. Noel, one of the great left-backs, switched to the centre of the Irish defence to try to stop Budgie's domination but Johnny was in untouchable mood. He was in complete control of the ball and ran the Irish defence dizzy.❞

Jimmy Greaves and Bobby were rested from the England team that destroyed the United States 10-0 in New York at the start of the summer tour, and got themselves in trouble with Alf Ramsey for sneaking off to watch First Lady of jazz Ella Fitzgerald in concert at Madison Square Garden. "Remember, I expect you to behave like my captain off as well as on the pitch," Alf told Bobby during a stern lecture ... and then named him as skipper for the next match against world champions Brazil.

CAP 22
Brazil, Rio de Janeiro, 30.5.64. England lost 5-1
Waiters Cohen Wilson Milne Norman Moore*
Thompson Greaves[1] Byrne J. Eastham Charlton R.

Highlights: Alf Ramsey preferred Tony Waiters to Gordon Banks in goal for this 'Little World Cup' tournament match against the world champions. Greaves equalized a first-half goal that Pele created for Rinaldo, and then midway through the second-half Pele took over and pulverized England with a purple patch that produced three goals in five minutes. Twice he earned free-kicks just outside the penalty area while dancing through the England defence juggling the ball like a circus performer. Waiters was completely deceived by swerving free-kicks from Rinaldo and Julinho, and then Pele contributed a magical goal of his own, pushing the ball through the legs of first Bobby Moore and then Maurice Norman before sending a long-range shot screaming into the net. Diaz scored goal number five after Pele had again confused the England defence two minutes from the end. Jimmy Greaves summed up the feelings of the England players when he said: 'Pele is on another bloody planet.'

BOBBY: ❝Pele was at his magical best, and it was almost a privilege to be on the same pitch. We kept him quiet for an hour and then he exploded into life and took us apart. He had everything, skill, speed, strength and was a master of ball control. He nutmegged me in one of his runs, and I considered it almost a badge of honour! I remember us wondering how we were going to win the World Cup in 1966 when Brazil were so clearly a better side ... and they had the one and only Pele.❞

CAP 23
Portugal, Sao Paulo, 4.6.64. Drew 1-1
Banks Thomson Wilson Flowers Norman Moore*
Paine Greaves Byrne J. Hunt[1] Thompson

Highlights: Portugal were down to ten men when centre-forward Jose Torres was sent off for attempting to hit the referee shortly after Roger Hunt had equalized a goal by Peres. Jimmy Greaves and Johnny Byrne hit the woodwork, and Byrne had a goal disallowed but England failed to take advantage of having an extra man. Had Torres landed with his attempted punch he could have faced a life ban from football. The trouble erupted after the referee disallowed a quite obviously off-side goal by Coluna. Portuguese players hounded the referee for a full five minutes, with Torres punished for being the ring leader. England had what looked a winner from Johnny Byrne turned down five minutes from the end and a bad-tempered match ended with a 1-1 scoreline that was a fair reflection of the play that was too often polluted by the threat of violence.

> *BOBBY:* ❛The night before this game we had been spectators at the Argentina/ Brazil match, and they kicked lumps out of each other. We sat on pitch-side benches, and had to make a run for our lives when the crowd turned their anger on us after Brazil had been beaten in a brutal battle. Portugal were a physically hard team but not as vicious as an Argentina side that took no prisoners. Pele was lucky to stay on after retaliating with a vicious tackle.❜

CAP 24
Argentina, Rio de Janeiro, 6.6.64. England lost 1-0
Banks Thomson Wilson Milne Norman Moore*
Thompson Greaves Byrne J. Eastham Charlton R.

Highlights: England held Argentina for an hour until Rojas scored in a breakaway raid seconds after the usually so reliable Greaves had missed a clear chance at the opposite end of the pitch. The Argentines, with skipper Antonio Rattin in commanding form, then played strolling possession football to frustrate England and to clinch victory in the 'Little World Cup' tournament. Argentina won the tournament with three wins from three matches, including victory over Brazil in a vicious game that was war masquerading as sport. England returned home convinced that Argentina would be the biggest mountain between them and the 1966 World Cup. They were particularly impressed by Rattin, the butter-smooth player who bossed the midfield with style and panache. He had a moment of madness when he disputed a decision by the referee. A hint of things to come!

Art Turner

A kiss for the FA Cup in 1964 at the start of Bobby's historic Wembley hat-trick

BOBBY: ❛Antonio Rattin was the player who impressed us most of all in that Little World Cup tournament. He was a big man, but graceful with it and while he seemed one paced, he had deceptive acceleration. Tall and commanding, he was Argentina's general and we were convinced he was going to be an influential player in the 1966 World Cup finals in England.❜

CAP 25
Northern Ireland, Windsor Park, 3.10.64. England won 4-3
Banks   Cohen Thomson Milne Norman Moore*
Paine   Greaves[3] Pickering[1] Charlton R. Thompson

Highlights: Master poacher Jimmy Greaves scored a first-half hat-trick as England rushed to a 4-0 half-time lead, but the second-half belonged to George Best and Ireland. The young Manchester United winger tied the defenders into knots, and inspired the Irish into a fight back that had England hanging on to a one goal lead at the final whistle. Alf Ramsey gave his team a rocket after the match for becoming complacent. If it had not been for a string of superb saves by Banks, Northern Ireland's second-half revival movement would have been rewarded with a remarkable victory. 'If we struggle to hold on to a 4-0 lead,' Ramsey said afterwards, 'what's going to happen if we go a goal down? We must start being more disciplined.'

BOBBY: ❛George was at his most magnificent and mischievous. He had us chasing shadows, and if it hadn't been for our English genius Jimmy Greaves we would have been bang in trouble. You would have thought at 4-0 up we were safe, but not when George Best is on the pitch and playing against you. He very nearly pulled it back on his own, and Alf gave us a real tongue lashing in the dressing-room afterwards. We all just had to shrug and accept that George was a bit special.❜

CAP 26
Belgium, Wembley, 21.10.64. Drew 2-2
Waiters   Cohen Thomson Milne Norman Moore*
Thompson Greaves   Pickering[1] Venables   Hinton[1]

Highlights: Ramsey experimented with a new left wing partnership of Terry Venables and Alan Hinton against a Belgian side that included eight players from their league champions Anderlecht. It was Hinton whose shot was deflected into the net for an equalizing goal in the seventieth minute. For Venables, selection completed a unique collection of England caps at all levels – schools, youth, amateur, Under-23 and full.

BOBBY: ‛Belgium featured one of my favourite players in Paul van Himst. I can never understand why he does not get more mentions when they talk about great inventive forwards. He was a real class act, and we really had our work cut out keeping him under control. It was the first time I had shaken hands at the toss-up with a captain – Jurion – wearing thick spectacles. We were fortunate to get away with a draw against a well-drilled side.’

Bobby was conspicuous by his absence from the next two England matches, and the reason was kept secret from all but a handful of trusted people. The West Ham and England captain had been struck by testicular cancer.

For the record, these were the two England games played while Bobby was going through a personal nightmare:

Wales, Wembley, 18.11.64. England won 2-1
Waiters Cohen Thomson Bailey Flowers*   Young
Thompson Hunt Wignall[2] Byrne J. Hinton

Highlights: Mike Bailey, Ron Flowers and Gerry Young formed a makeshift half-back line because of injuries. There was also an experimental inside-forward trio, with Frank Wignall the spearhead to Roger Hunt and Johnny Byrne. Nottingham Forest centre-forward Wignall scored both England goals before Cliff Jones netted for Wales. There were only 40,000 spectators at Wembley, and the game lacked atmosphere and direction.

Holland, Amsterdam 9.12.64. Drew 1-1
Waiters Cohen Thomson Mullery Norman Flowers*
Thompson Greaves[1] Wignall Venables Charlton R.

Highlights: Alan Mullery made his debut in midfield alongside Terry Venables, a partnership that they would soon renew at Tottenham. They combined to create a goal for another Spurs star, Jimmy Greaves, who scored four minutes from the end to force a draw in this match to celebrate the 75th anniversary of the Dutch FA. England played the game at exhibition pace as if they did not want to spoil the Dutch party. Maurice Norman, the big ox of a centre-half who had been like a man mountain in the middle of the Tottenham and England defences, broke a leg in a meaningless club friendly against Hungary and his distinguished career for club and country was over. This opened the door for the arrival on the international stage of the Giraffe, Jack Charlton.

Chapter 7: The Secret Operation

NOTHING more dramatically illustrates the change in the approach to cancer than Bobby's nightmare experience in the autumn of 1964. It was a closely guarded secret that when he went into hospital it was for the surgical removal of a testicle that had become cancerous. England's finest young footballer was desperately worried by a life-threatening disease, and only a handful of people knew.

It was dismissed for public consumption as a minor groin problem, and routine treatment for an injury picked up on the football field while playing for West Ham. Those few of us in the media who knew the horrifying truth kept quiet about it. This was private territory, and we just wanted Bobby to get through his ordeal and return to the game in which he was now established as a major player. Covering up a story of such weight today would, quite rightly, get the reporter the sack. But back in the 1960s cancer was a word to be whispered, and euphemistically dismissed with a Les Dawson-style mime as 'the Big C.'

Bobby became a huge hero in the world of football without anybody knowing the personal mountain he climbed. Can you imagine his hero status if people had realised that he had come through such a serious cancer operation before his greatest feat of leading England to the World Cup? He would have been the perfect role model for people affected by the disease, but those of us around at the time will confirm that it was a taboo subject in the 'sixties and it was all hushed up. Only years later we learned of the agony he went through, crying in the arms of his seven-months-pregnant wife Tina when he first realised the extent of his problem. The drama is graphically captured in the book Tina wrote in harness with top sportswriter Julie Welch. You would never have got Bobby to admit that he had been reduced to tears. His enormous pride would not have allowed that confession.

It is the saddest of facts that a more virulent form of cancer would come back to haunt and finally defeat our hero, but back in the summertime of his great footballing career most people just did not have an inkling of his ordeal and suffering. How everybody would have saluted Bobby if only they had known of his courageous struggle, and all this time his wife Tina was waiting to give birth to their first baby. The gorgeous Roberta arrived on January 24 1965, by which time Bobby was back on the football roundabout and with his testicle-removing operation still a secret from most of the world. There were just a few footballing mates who knew the truth:

I was lost in admiration for the way Bobby handled his problem. There were just a handful of us who knew what he had been through, but he never once complained and just got on with proving himself the greatest defender in the game. I am sure if the public had known he'd had a testicle removed they would have been even more impressed by the way he played both for club and country. He had to show enormous character to get over an experience that would have destroyed the confidence of a lesser man. I was always a fan of Bobby's and tried hard to sign him for Norwich at the back end of his career. If there has been a better defender in an England shirt I have not seen him.

CAP 27

Scotland, Wembley, 10.4.65. Drew 2-2

Banks Cohen Wilson Stiles Charlton J. Moore*
Thompson Greaves[1] Bridges Byrne J. Charlton R.[1]

Highlights: England, with Bobby Moore back as skipper after his secret testicular cancer operation, did well to salvage a draw from a game in which they were reduced to only nine fit players. Ray Wilson went off at half-time with torn rib muscles, and Johnny Byrne – dropping back to replace Wilson in defence – became a limping passenger with a knee injury that virtually finished his international career. Ramsey blooded Barry Bridges, Nobby Stiles and Jack Charlton (with brother Bobby on the left wing). This was the first time that England's 1966 World Cup defence paraded together. Bobby Charlton and Jimmy Greaves gave England a commanding 2-0 lead inside the first thirty-five minutes. Denis Law scored for Scotland five minutes before half-time with a viciously swerving shot, and Ian St John equalized midway through the second-half after Cohen had cleared a Davie Wilson shot off the line.

BOBBY: **❝**I was devastated for my mate Johnny Byrne, who was obviously badly injured and was in awful pain after the match. Alf was saying publicly that we would win the World Cup, but we knew we had to improve on this performance against Scotland. We let a 2-0 lead go, but the injuries robbed us of our early rhythm and we were clinging on at the end.**❞**

Johnny Byrne, a ball-playing maestro whose England career was cut short by injury

CAP 28
Hungary, Wembley, 5.5.65. England won 1-0
Banks   Cohen Wilson Stiles   Charlton J. Moore*
Paine   Greaves[1] Bridges Eastham Connelly

Highlights: Alf Ramsey's international playing career had ended the last time the Hungarians visited Wembley for their famous 6-3 victory in 1953. His long-awaited revenge was given to him by a well-constructed Jimmy Greaves goal in the sixteenth minute. Bobby Charlton failed a late fitness test and John Connelly was recalled for the first time since Ramsey's desperate first match against France. England's attacking moves were often disjointed and lacking imagination, but the most heartening sight for Ramsey was seeing the defence comfortably cope with a Hungarian forward line that was not a patch on their predecessors of 1953.

> *BOBBY:* ❛I had never seen Alf so happy after a victory. It was as if the win over Hungary had cleared a skeleton out of his cupboard. I was a football-daft kid of twelve when the Magical Magyars put six goals past England goalkeeper Gil Merrick in 1953, and could not believe the result. I thought we were unbeatable at Wembley. What was most satisfying about the 1965 performance was that our defence was solid and unbeaten against a talented attack.❜

CAP 29
Yugoslavia, Belgrade, 9.5.65. Drew 1-1
Banks   Cohen Wilson   Stiles   Charlton J. Moore*
Paine   Greaves Bridges[1] Ball   Connelly

Highlights: Ramsey's jigsaw came closer to completion when Blackpool's irrepressible Alan Ball made his debut, showing the energy and enthusiasm that was to make him such a vital member of the 1966 World Cup squad. Barry Bridges, Chelsea's jet-paced centre-forward, headed England's equaliser after the Yugoslavs had taken a fifteenth minute lead. England were the first foreign side to avoid defeat in Yugoslavia in a full international. "It's the proudest moment of my life," said Ballie in his Clitheroe Kid high-pitch voice after Ramsey had selected him. "I have dreamed of playing for my country ever since I first kicked a ball. There can be no greater honour. I would willingly play for nothing."

> *BOBBY:* ❛ I have never known any player as enthusiastic as Ballie. He lifted the entire team with his energy and sheer joy of playing. He was only a baby in football terms but had an old head on those young shoulders, and he had a good tactical brain to go with his skill.❜

J UST six months after his testicular cancer operation, Bobby climbed the 39 steps at Wembley to collect the European Cup Winners' Cup following West Ham's 2-0 victory over Munich 1860 in a classic final. It was a performance that Ron Greenwood described with justification as "close to perfection."

West Ham fans feared that their attack would not be firing on all cylinders because of the injury-forced absence of dribbling winger Peter Brabrook and highly skilled centre-forward Budgie Byrne. But within minutes their local hero stand-ins, Alan Sealey and Brian Dear, were making deep and daring inroads into the much-vaunted Munich defence.

With Bobby Moore majestic at the back, West Ham were always looking the side most likely to conquer and two goals in ninety seconds by Sealey virtually clinched victory with twenty minutes to go.

> *BOBBY:* ❛I was so proud to be part of that performance. It was a real team effort, with everybody working together. Munich had four West German internationals and went into the match hot favourites, but we refused to let them dominate and were good value for our win. As Ron Greenwood said, 'If you want to know about West Ham's footballing philosophy judge us on this match.'❜

For the record, West Ham's winning team: Standen, Bond, Burkett, Peters, Brown, Moore Sealey[2], Boyce, Hurst, Dear, Sissons. It was a sporting contest played in good spirit and the two clubs later shared a United Nations Fair Play award for their conduct. Meantime, Bobby was leading England in their match preparations building up to the 1966 World Cup.

CAP 32
Wales, Ninian Park, 2.10.65. Drew 0-0
Springett Cohen Wilson Stiles Charlton J.   Moore*
Paine   Greaves Peacock Charlton R. Connelly

Highlights: Goalkeeper Ron Springett was recalled for his first game since his nightmare match in France in Ramsey's first game as England manager. He played impressively enough in a goalless game to book a place in the 1966 World Cup squad as an understudy to his successor Gordon Banks. Fielding six players from outside the First Division, Wales managed to prevent England from scoring for the first time in thirty-three years. They had the most productive player on the pitch in balding, 35-year-old Ivor Allchurch, an artist of a player who always managed to put the correct weight to his passes even now that he was into the autumn of his career and playing with Swansea in the Third Division.

BOBBY: ❛I was so pleased for Ron Springett, keeping a blank sheet. He was desperately unlucky to lose his place after his performance against France in Alf's first game. The conditions were appalling and Ron kept losing the ball under the poor floodlights. But all of us in the game knew he was a class act, and he proved in this match that he was an ideal understudy for the great Gordon Banks.❜

CAP 33
Austria, Wembley, 20.10.65. England lost 3-2
Springett   Cohen Wilson Stiles   Charlton J.   Moore*
Paine   Greaves   Bridges Charlton R.[1] Connelly[1]

Highlights: England were twice in front through Bobby Charlton and John Connelly, but slack defensive play let the Austrians in for two late goals. It was to be England's last defeat before the World Cup, and ended an unbeaten run of nine games. The Austrians, the third overseas team to win at Wembley, were flattered by their victory, and the result did not dent Alf Ramsey's confidence that England were going to win the World Cup.

BOBBY: ❛Greavsie, of all people, missed a hat-trick of simple chances, and seemed strangely listless. He was later diagnosed as suffering from hepatitis and was out of the game for the next five months. Jimmy worked wonders to get himself fit for the World Cup campaign.❜

CAP 34
Northern Ireland, Wembley, 10.11.65. England won 2-1
Banks   Cohen Wilson Stiles   Charlton J.   Moore*
Thompson   Baker[1]   Peacock[1]   Charlton R.   Connelly

Highlights: Joe Baker, deputising for the hospitalized Greaves, put England in the lead in the nineteenth minute. The Irish equalised sixty seconds later when Willie Irvine turned a George Best centre through the legs of an embarrassed Banks. Persistent rain made the surface treacherous, and the Irish defenders were slithering around when Alan Peacock scored England's winner in the seventieth minute. Under gentle persuasion from Alf Ramsey – and at club level, Matt Busby – Bobby Charlton was starting to specialize in more of a withdrawn role, and he was developing into the Great Conductor.

> *BOBBY*: ‘I remember Bobby Charlton breaking into the England team as a bombing inside-forward and then as a left winger with a rocket shot, and now he was playing a more subtle game as a deep-lying centre-forward. He was a fantastic player in every role and one of the all-time greats. We were very lucky to have a forward of his calibre to call on.’

CAP 35
Spain, Madrid, 8.12.65. England won 2-0
Banks   Cohen Wilson   Stiles Charlton J. Moore*
Ball   Hunt[1] Baker[1] (Hunter)   Eastham   Charlton R.

Highlights: One of the most significant games in Alf Ramsey's managerial life. He gave full rein to his 4-3-3 formation for the first time following the experiment in Nuremburg, and the resounding victory convinced him that he had found the tactics best suited to England for the World Cup. The defence was as it would appear throughout the World Cup finals – Banks behind a back line of Cohen, Jack Charlton, Moore and Wilson. Stiles patrolled the midfield as a ball winner alongside the fetch and carrying Alan Ball, with George Eastham orchestrating things from a deep position in centre midfield (the role that would eventually become Bobby Charlton's). Here in Spain Bobby wore the number eleven shirt and was delegated an attacking role alongside out-and-out strikers Roger Hunt and Joe Baker, who spoke with such a heavy Scottish accent that many of his colleagues could not always understand him. It was Baker who gave England an early lead on a pitch soaked by melting snow before limping off in the thirty-fifth minute with a pulled muscle. Norman 'Bites Yer Legs' Hunter became the first England player to make his debut as a substitute. Roger Hunt clinched victory with a classic goal on the hour after a sweeping length-of-the-pitch passing movement involving George Cohen, Bobby Charlton and Bobby Moore. The Liverpool striker was making a strong challenge for the England shirt usually worn by the absent, unwell Greaves.

> *BOBBY*: ‘As Norman Hunter came on, Ballie put his hands together and said; 'For what they are about to receive …!' In fairness, there was a lot more to Norman's game than his fierce tackling. He could use the ball intelligently and accurately with that left foot of his. We were all excited by this victory, because we knew we had a new formation that worked.’

**EYEWITNESS
ALAN
BALL**

The win in Madrid gave a huge lift to our confidence, and we began to agree with Alf – we could win the World Cup. We had all the ingredients, great players, a great captain and now a great system. The fact that we also had home advantage meant everything was just right as we came into the World Cup year. I was always a huge fan of Bobby's. He was a magnificent defender and led by example. Walking out on to the pitch behind him made you feel ten feet tall. He became a very close friend and I was so proud to have him as a team-mate and as a pal.

CAP 36
Poland, Liverpool, 5.1.66. Drew 1-1
Banks Cohen Wilson Stiles   Charlton J. Moore*[1]
Ball   Hunt   Baker Eastham Harris

Highlights: Bobby Moore scored one of the two goals that decorated his 108 international appearances to cancel out Poland's lead on a glue-pot pitch at Goodison. Moore put the finishing touch to a late move started by Burnley winger Gordon Harris, deputising for the injured Bobby Charlton, and it was Jack Charlton who made the final pass that created the opening for England's skipper. This was the first match between England and Poland, and the first full international for 13 years at a Goodison ground that was to be one of the World Cup venues. Incessant rain turned the pitch into a quagmire that made every step a challenge. No doubt buoyed by his rare goal, Moore stormed into the penalty area in the closing minutes to meet a centre from the tireless Alan Ball and powered a header against the crossbar. Again, Alf Ramsey played 4-3-3, with Stiles, Ball and Eastham working together in midfield.

BOBBY: ❛Goodison was in the worst condition I'd ever known it, and it was difficult to move the ball about. Big Jack Charlton gave the pass for my goal and said we were the new secret-weapon strike force. Then Ballie called me the new Tommy Lawton when I headed against the bar. We were developing a fantastic team spirit. It was just like playing for a club side.❜

CAP 37
West Germany, Wembley, 23.2.66. England won 1-0
Banks Cohen Newton (Wilson) Moore* Charlton J. Hunter
Ball   Hunt   Stiles[1] Hurst Charlton R.

Highlights: This was to prove a dress rehearsal for the World Cup final just five months later. Nobby Stiles, wearing the number nine shirt but playing in midfield, scored the only goal of the match and of his international career. Some of the less educated football reporters wrote that Stiles had played at centre-forward and that 'Ramsey's gamble of playing him as a spearhead' paid off with a goal. They were yet to understand that shirt numbers were becoming meaningless. Little had been learned since back in the 1950s when Nandor Hidegkuti completely baffled England's defence by playing a withdrawn role in the number nine shirt. Geoff Hurst made an impressive England debut, and Keith Newton's first England game ended just before half-time when he limped off to be replaced by substitute Ray Wilson. The Germans claimed an equaliser when Heiss turned in a cross from Held, but the referee disallowed it after consulting a flag-waving linesman. The shape of things to come! The appearance together of Stiles and Hunter meant the game became a bruise on the memory of several of the Germans.

BOBBY: ❛When Nobby scored, his best mate Alan Ball said, 'Don't make a note of the time of the goal but the date ... it's historic.' What with me scoring our only goal in the previous match against Poland, we defenders were giving our forwards terrible stick. It was great to have my West Ham team-mate Geoff Hurst in the England team. And Martin Peters was waiting in the wings.❜

CAP 38
Scotland, Hampden Park, 2.4.66. England won 4-3
Banks Cohen Newton Stiles   Charlton J. Moore*
Ball   Hunt[2] Charlton R.[1] Hurst[1] Connelly

Highlights: Geoff Hurst scored his first goal for England in the nineteenth minute to start a spree that excited the 133,000 crowd but made purists wince at the procession of defensive blunders by both teams. Hunt added a second goal for England before Denis Law threw himself forward in typical dare-devil style to head Scotland's first goal just before half-time. Hunt made it 3-1 early in the second-half, and then Celtic's jinking winger Jimmy Johnstone pulled it back to 3-2 before a thunderbolt shot from Bobby Charlton restored the two-goal lead. This was Charlton in imperious form as he reveled in his role as midfield orchestrator. Johnstone, turning the England defence inside out with his dribbling runs, scored the final goal six minutes from the end with a delicate curling shot that deceived goalkeeper Gordon Banks.

BOBBY: ❛I winced when a journalist said to Alf immediately after the match, 'A great game to watch, Alf.' That was not Alf's view. 'For you maybe,' he said, 'but I thought there was some appalling football played. We must be much, much tighter.' Seven-goal thrillers did not belong in Alf's textbook. Once a perfectionist right-back, always a perfectionist right-back.❜

As Alf experimented in the final build-up to the World Cup, he rested Bobby against Yugoslavia and Finland, with Jimmy Armfied returning as skipper. The village world of football buzzed with rumours that Alf was going to leave the West Ham captain out of his starting eleven for the World Cup.

BOBBY: ❛If it was Alf's idea to gee me up, it certainly worked. I silently vowed that if I got back into the team I would never give him an excuse to leave me out again. Alf always played things close to his chest, and no player could be over confident. There was no such thing as an automatic place.❜

For the record, these were the England teams and match highlights for the games against Yugoslavia and Finland:

Yugoslavia, Wembley, 4.5.66. England won 2-0
Banks Armfield* Wilson   Peters   Charlton J. Hunter
Paine   Greaves[1]   Charlton R.[1] Hurst Tambling

Highlights: Jimmy Greaves, back in the England team after his hepatitis-forced five-month lay-off, scored the first goal in the ninth minute. Bobby Charlton celebrated being elected 'Footballer of the Year' by wrapping up England's victory with another of his screaming long-range shots. Martin Peters, the player who would be described by Ramsey as 'ten years ahead of his time', twice went close to marking his debut with a goal against a highly skilled Yugoslav side. It was England's last home game before the World Cup and they responded with a powerful performance that sent a mood of optimism shooting through the country.

Finland, Helsinki, 26.6.66. England won 3-0
Banks Armfield* Wilson Peters[1]   Charlton J.[1] Hunter
Callaghan Hunt[1] Charlton R. Hurst Ball

Highlights: Martin Peters scored his first goal for England and the first of the match at the start of a final warm-up tour before the World Cup finals. Alan Ball failed from the penalty spot in a game remembered more for the many missed chances than those that were eventually taken by Roger Hunt and Jack Charlton.

CAP 39
Norway, Oslo, 29.6.66. England won 6-1
Springett   Cohen Byrne G. Stiles   Flowers Moore*[1]
Paine   Greaves[4] Charlton R. Hunt Connelly[1]

Highlights: Jimmy Greaves scored four goals for the second time in his international career against a Norwegian team that was out of its depth. A misplaced back pass by Ron Flowers gifted the Norwegians a fourth minute lead, but from then on England totally dominated play. Greaves scored all his goals in the first-half and was now top England goalscorer with 43 goals from 49 international matches. Bobby Moore got on the scoresheet with a twenty-five yard drive that could have come from the boot of Bobby Charlton, who created the sixth goal for John Connelly in a second-half played at exhibition pace. FA and Chelsea chairman Joe Mears, a long-time friend and sup-porter of Greaves, died of a heart attack in Oslo the day after the match, which threw a blanket of despair over the entire squad. Mears, 'Mr Chelsea', had been a driving force in the preparations for England's hosting of the World Cup finals.

> *BOBBY*: "It was marvellous to see Greavsie back in full flow after his illness. He was my best mate in football, and without any argument the greatest English goal scorer since the war. I was thrilled with my goal, a long-range shot that was a goal from the moment it left my boot. I was pleased to be able to tell Jimmy that he had never scored a goal from that range for England. Quietly, I was very relieved to be back in the team. It was a tragedy to lose Joe Mears. He was a true gentleman, and loved every second of his football whether with England or Chelsea."

CAP 40
Denmark, Copenhagen, 3.7.66. England won 2-0
Bonetti Cohen Wilson Stiles   Charlton J.[1] Moore*
Ball   Greaves Hurst Eastham[1] Connelly

Highlights: Goals from Jack Charlton and George Eastham gave England their sixth successive victory. Chelsea goalkeeper Peter Bonetti had his first taste of international football and performed well on a bumpy pitch that led to many errors in front of him. The amateurs of Denmark, playing for their pride, were robust with their challenges. This brought out the vicious competitive edge that lurked just below the surface with Nobby Stiles and Alan Ball, and they were both given lectures by the Canadian referee for wild tackles that bordered on the unacceptable. Jimmy Greaves, four-goal hero in the previous match, hardly got a touch of the ball in his milestone fiftieth international game.

BOBBY: ❝The Danes played as if this was their World Cup final, and they took no prisoners. We were up against a nine-man defence for much of the game, and we were glad to get off the pitch in one piece. Jack Charlton was jokingly claiming he should be leading the attack after another of his smash-and-grab goals.❞

CAP 41
Poland, Chorzow, 5.7.66. England won 1-0
Banks Cohen Wilson Stiles Charlton J. Moore*
Ball   Greaves Charlton R. Hunt[1] Peters

Highlights: A beautifully struck shot by Roger Hunt in the thirteenth minute was enough to give England victory in this final match before the World Cup finals. This would prove to be the team that just twenty-five days later captured the World Cup for England, with just one exception: Hurst in place of Greaves. Alf Ramsey had unveiled his wingless wonders, and there is no doubt that he considered this his strongest line-up. Martin Peters was the man of the match, sharing scheming duties with Bobby Charlton, and having the energy to help out in both defence and attack whenever necessary. He did it all with style and grace, and it was a surprise when he failed to make Ramsey's team for the opening match of the World Cup six days later.

BOBBY: ❝Alf had brought us to the boil at just the right time, and we were all desperate for the World Cup to start. Martin Peters had a magnificent game and looked odds on to have won a place in the team for the first match, so it came as a shock when Alf announced the side with Martin left out.❞

Now everything was all set for the World Cup finals and the kick-off at Wembley, with Bobby confirmed as the man with the honour of leading England out for the greatest football show on earth.

Then, dramatically with less than a week to go, news broke that Alf Ramsey had been warned he may have to go into the tournament without his skipper. The nation caught its breath.

Chapter 9: They Think It's All Over

BOBBY went into the World Cup under a cloud of confusion. He was in a contract dispute with West Ham and had refused to re-sign in the hope that Tottenham would follow up on their barely secret interest in him. Both Terry Venables and Jimmy Greaves had quietly tipped off Bobby that manager Bill Nicholson wanted him at White Hart Lane, but Hammers were determined to hold on to their captain.

The Football Association made it clear to Alf Ramsey that an unregistered player would not be eligible to take part in the World Cup. Ron Greenwood, with whom Bobby now had a frosty relationship, was summoned to the England team headquarters at the last minute to sign his skipper on a one-month contract.

BOBBY: ❛You have to remember that at the time Tottenham had one of the best teams in Europe, and I was concerned that I was getting stale at West Ham. I felt almost as if I was being blackmailed into signing a contract, but we compromised and agreed to renegotiate once the World Cup was over. I wanted to give the tournament every ounce of my energy and concentration. Let's face it, for me it was the biggest challenge of my life.❜

It was a mightily relieved Alf Ramsey who was able to name Bobby as his captain for the opening match of the 1966 World Cup ...

CAP 42
Uruguay, World Cup, Wembley, 11.7.66. Drew 0-0
Banks Cohen Wilson Stiles Charlton J.   Moore*
Ball Greaves Charlton R. Hunt Connelly

Highlights: A dull and uninspiring start to the World Cup left neutrals wondering on what Alf Ramsey based his confidence that England would win the tournament. Uruguay played with nine men back in defence and defied all England's attempts to break them down. It was the first time in twelve matches that England had failed to score. John Connelly was Ramsey's one winger. The Uruguayans celebrated at the final whistle as if they had won. They had squeezed exactly what they wanted from the game.

BOBBY: 'We were very flat at the end of the game because we knew we hadn't delivered. There was only one team trying to play, and it wasn't Uruguay. They just came to stifle us and did not allow our forwards time or space to breathe. I remember Ballie throwing his boots on the dressing-room floor in disgust and saying in that high-pitched voice of his, 'If I go for a sh*t, I'm expecting two Uruguayans to come with me.' It could only get better.'

CAP 43
Mexico, World Cup, Wembley, 16.7.66. England won 2-0

Banks   Cohen   Wilson   Stiles   Charlton J. Moore*
Paine   Greaves   Charlton R.[1]   Hunt[1]   Peters

Highlights: Alf Ramsey had not yet completely abandoned wingers. Terry Paine was preferred to Connelly in this second game, with Martin Peters taking the place of Alan Ball in midfield. Bobby Charlton unleashed one of his magnificent twenty-five yard specials for the first goal, and Roger Hunt clinched victory after having what looked a good goal ruled off-side. After the frustration of the opening match against Uruguay, this victory convinced many people that England could live up to Ramsey's expectations. Mexico were not allowed to create a single goal-scoring chance by an England defence in which Bobby Moore was at his commanding best.

BOBBY: 'We made a stuttering start but our nerves settled once Bobby scored with one of his rockets. Ballie was heartbroken to be left out and we had to rally round him to stop him walking out. We knew there was plenty more to come from him. We were really feeling the pressure of being the host country, but this victory helped lift us and the supporters.'

CAP 44
France, World Cup, Wembley, 20.7.66. England won 2-0

Banks   Cohen   Wilson   Stiles   Charlton J. Moore*
Callaghan   Greaves   Charlton R.   Hunt[2]   Peters

Highlights: Two smartly taken Roger Hunt goals gave England a confidence booster on their way into the World Cup quarter-finals. Ian Callaghan became the third winger tried by the England manager. Jimmy Greaves finished the match with a deep gash on his left shin, and Stiles was booked for a crunching tackle on French striker Simon. He was fortunate not to be sent off, and Ramsey ignored calls from Football Association officials that he should drop Stiles because of his competitive nature. 'If Stiles goes, so do I,' said Ramsey. And he was not feigning.

BOBBY: ❝Alf was furious when the Blazers tried to put pressure on him to drop Nobby. He knew how vital his ball-winning performances were to the team in an era when fierce tackling midfield players were necessary. The way Alf stood by Nobby helped strengthen the bond in the England camp and we were growing in confidence by the minute.❞

CAP 45
Argentina, World Cup, Wembley, 23.7.66. England won 1-0
Banks Cohen Wilson Stiles   Charlton J. Moore*
Ball Hurst[1]   Charlton R.   Hunt   Peters

Highlights: Argentina shelved their superior skills and instead concentrated on what seemed a premeditated policy of disrupting England with a spate of petty fouls. Their captain Antonio Rattin arrogantly challenged just about every decision that the referee made and was waving his arms around like a traffic policeman. Finally the referee, a balding, little West German called Rudlof Kreitlin, could take no more of Rattin's disruptive tactics and ordered him off. It was almost comical to see the tiny figure of the referee staring up at the tall, stately looking Rattin and demanding that he leave the field. It was also very sad. It took nine minutes of argument and touchline inter-pretations before Rattin finally walked. Geoff Hurst, making his debut in place of the injured Greaves, headed the winning goal from a Martin Peters cross to the near post. It was a classical creation that had made-in-West Ham written all over it. For Gordon Banks, it was a record seventh successive England appearance without conceding a goal. This was the first match in which England played without a recognised winger. Ramsey's 'Wingless Wonders' were off the launching pad. Alan Ball, so disappointed to miss the previous two matches that he considered walking out, gave a perpetual motion performance that confirmed that he was in the side to stay. Alf Ramsey described the Argentinians as 'animals', a heat-of-the-moment description that had diplomatic reper-cussions and led to official protests being made to the British ambassador in Buenos Aires. The sad fact is that Argentina were the most skilful side in the tournament, but they allowed their tempers to over-rule their talent.

BOBBY: ❝I'd never known Alf as angry. He nearly blew a gasket when George Cohen tried to swap shirts with one of the Argentinians. I was thrilled with the part my West Ham team-mates had played in the victory. Geoff's goal came from a near-post move that we had perfected at Upton Park. We knew what to expect from Argentina because we'd seen them against Brazil a year earlier. Rattin was a flawed genius, a marvellous footballer but he lost his discipline. I had learned long ago to control my temper.❞

CAP 46
Portugal, World Cup, Wembley, 26.7.66. England won 2-1
Banks   Cohen Wilson Stiles   Charlton J. Moore*
Ball   Hurst   Charlton R.[2] Hunt Peters

Highlights: This was THE classic match of the 1966 World Cup. It lacked the drama of the Final, but the football played by both teams had rarely been bettered at Wembley. The match belonged more to Bobby Charlton than anybody. He moved with the grace of a Nureyev on grass and the power of a panther. His reward was two superb goals, one drilled low into the net from a rebound after a Roger Hunt shot had been blocked, and the second, a real beauty, rifled high into the net from twenty-five yards. Seven minutes from the end England's magnificent defence conceded their first goal of the tournament when Eusebio scored from the penalty spot after Jack Charlton had handled a header from Jose Torres. Nobby Stiles performed a disciplined containing role on the great Eusebio, fresh from his stunning four-goal performance against North Korea in the quarter-final at Goodison after the Koreans had rushed three goals into the lead. Eusebio left the pitch in tears as the two teams got a standing ovation for producing a match that would live long in the memory.

BOBBY: ❛This was the performance that finally convinced our critics and our supporters that we had the skill, the determination and the all-round talent to win the World Cup. The game belonged to Manchester United. Bobby scored two cracking goals and Nobby did a brilliant job snuffing out the great Eusebio. Nobody could complain that he kept Eusebio quiet with anything but good old-fashioned man marking, always snapping at his heels and making sure he had no room for his electric spurts. There was nothing in the slightest bit dirty or violent about the job he did. It was just great, disciplined defending. We were choked to concede a goal, but had still not let one in in open play. Banksie was having a magnificent tournament and apologised for not saving Eusebio's penalty! I had a bit of a worry after the match when I was diagnosed with tonsilitis, but some tablets from our medic Doc Bass quickly controlled it.❜

CAP 47
West Germany, World Cup Final, Wembley, 30.7.66. England won 4-2 (aet)
Banks   Cohen Wilson Stiles   Charlton J. Moore*
Ball   Hurst[3] Charlton R.   Hunt Peters[1]

Highlights: Alf Ramsey decided to stick with an unchanged team. No place for fit-again Jimmy Greaves, who spent the morning of the match packing his bags for a quick

Bobby on top of the world ... on the shoulders of Geoff Hurst and Ray Wilson

getaway to a family holiday. Alf had said nothing to him, but he guessed he would be missing out on the game of a lifetime. West Germany took the negative approach of putting Beckenbauer on man-to-man marking duty against Bobby Charlton, so the two most creative players on the pitch cancelled each other out. This was manager Helmut Schoen's reaction to Charlton's spectacular show against Portugal. A rare Ray Wilson mistake on a wet surface let Helmut Haller in for a 13th minute goal which was equalised six minutes later when Hurst headed in a perfectly flighted free-kick from his West Ham team-mate Bobby Moore. Just after the hour a Hurst shot was blocked and it was another West Hammer, Martin Peters, who smacked the rebound smartly into the net to make it 2-1. England were one minute from the World Cup when Jack Charlton was adjudged to have fouled Germany's skipper Uwe Seeler. During a goalmouth scramble that followed the free-kick defender Wolfgang Weber forced the ball into the net, with skipper Moore insisting there had been a handball. Ten minutes into extra-time, the inexhaustible Alan Ball made one of his many scampering runs past left-back Schnellinger and centered the ball. Hurst turned and fired a first-time shot against the under-side of the bar, and as it bounced down England claimed the ball had crossed the goal-line. Swiss referee Gottfried Dienst awarded a controversial goal after consulting the Russian linesman Bakhramov. To this day, the Germans dispute the decision. Hurst ended all arguments in the final seconds when he ran on to a perfect pass from Moore and hammered a left foot shot past goalkeeper Hans Tilkowski to complete the first ever World Cup hat-trick. It presented the BBC's Kenneth Wolstenholme with one of the most memorable of all commentary lines: "Some people are on the pitch ... they think it's all over ... it is now!" England were champions of the world.

BOBBY: ❝I was heartbroken for my room-mate Greavsie that he missed out, but at the same time pleased for my clubmate Geoff. My opinion was that Jimmy would have frightened the life out of the Germans with his finishing skill, but I knew there was no way Alf could change a winning team after our performance against Portugal. The game should never have gone to extra-time. Their last minute free-kick should have been awarded to England because Seeler made a back for Jack Charlton. Then as the ball bounced around the penalty area like a pinball Schnellinger definitely handled it before Weber bundled the ball into the net. Alf was magnificent. He wasn't panicking or shouting. He just said, plainly and simply, 'You've won the World Cup once ... now go out and do it again.' He pointed to the German players. 'Look at them,' he said. 'They are out on their feet. Now finish them off.' I was too far away to judge whether Geoff's extra-time shot had crossed the line, but Roger Hunt was on the spot and immediately turned in celebration of a goal. He is a good honest man, and that convinced me it was right to award the goal. Then Geoff settled all arguments with his fantastic hat-trick goal.❞

EYEWITNESS JACK CHARLTON

Bobby Moore was magnificent throughout the 1966 World Cup. If anybody wants to know why he was a class apart, just watch the moments before Geoff Hurst completed his hat-trick in the '66 final. There were only seconds to go and Bobby was in possession deep in England's half. I shouted for him to belt the bloody ball clear and put it in row Z, anything to waste time. But Bobby, as usual, kept his head, dribbled the ball forward and paused and looked up to see where his West Ham team-mate Geoff Hurst was. He then played an inch-perfect thirty-yard pass right into Geoff's path, when anybody else would have hoofed it out of play. Geoff went on to score his match-clinching third goal. It was an astonishing bit of artistry from Bobby when you consider the circumstances. He was a real thoroughbred.

The always meticulous, always calculating, always immaculate Bobby Moore was even thinking better than anybody else as he climbed the 39 steps at Wembley for a third successive year. He noticed that the Queen – waiting to present him with the Jules Rimet trophy – was wearing white gloves, and he had the presence of mind to wipe his hands on the velvet drapes decorating the Royal Box rather than get mud on them. Talk about On Her Majesty's Secret Laundry Service.

After all the shooting and the shouting was over the world's press were invited to vote for the outstanding player of the tournament.

Eusebio was top scorer with nine goals, Gordon Banks had been a marvellous goalkeeper, Bobby Charlton explosive with his finishing, young Franz Beckenbauer exceptional in the German team. But there could be only one winner, a player who had led the England team with dignity, elegance and a composure and confidence that put him on a pedestal above all others.

The Player of the 1966 World Cup was, of course, the blond boy from Barking, Bobby Moore. His reward was a £1000 bonus from the vote organisers, Radox Bath Salts. He was forever blowing bubbles.

Chapter 10: The businessman

ONCE Operation World Cup had been successfully completed, Bobby negotiated a lucrative new deal with West Ham. But things were never quite the same again between him and the man who had been his football mentor, Ron Greenwood. They jelled on playing matters, but had little in common away from the training ground. The Lancastrian-born manager was almost amateur in his outlook and ideals. He had been a professional footballer in the days when the most that players earned was £17 a week, and he was never comfortable with the new riches pouring into the game. In contrast, Bobby always knew his worth as a player.

Suddenly he was earning £150 a week, a huge wage in the 1960s, and his agent Jack Turner – the man who first assessed him for West Ham – was inundated with commercial propositions. Under Turner's guidance, he opened a Bobby Moore Sports Shop opposite the Upton Park ground, made a series of television commercials, put his name to magazine and newspaper columns, and was in demand for personal appearances, endorsements and sportswear sponsorship. He and Tina moved into a beautiful home in Chigwell, bought a place in Marbella and later had a sumptuous Essex mansion – Moorlands – built for a then staggering £100,000. He was mixing in showbusiness circles miles away from the world of Ron Greenwood, and included among his close friends the likes of Jimmy Tarbuck, Kenny Lynch and the then James Bond, Sean Connery. Ron considered most not involved in the game as hangers-on.

Bobby became an ambitious but never lucky businessman, putting money and energy into a series of enterprises including a suede and leatherware factory, Bobby Moore jewellery, a shirt-making company part-owned by Manchester City winger Mike Summerbee, and several London pubs that brought him nothing but headaches.

He went into the pub business with his Chigwell neighbour Jimmy Quill, with whom I had gone to Raine's Grammar school in Stepney. We used to call him 'Jimmy the Jab', because he won schoolboy boxing titles with a wickedly fast left jab. Among the pubs he went on to own was the notorious Blind Beggar, just a stroll from our old school where Ronnie Kray shot dead another gangster, George Cornell.

Jimmy and Bobby opened Mooro's in Stratford, and his hugely gifted Fulham clubmates Rodney Marsh and George Best were among the celebrities at the grand opening. George and Bobby were close friends off the pitch, and greatly admired each

Opening night at Mooro's in Stratford, November 1976, from left to right: Rodney Marsh, Kenny Lynch, Frank Lampard Snr, Alan Ball, George Best, Malcolm Macdonald and mine host, Mooro.

other as footballers. Their drinking sessions became the source of much-exaggerated legend. Unexplained fires at two of the pubs in which Bobby had invested ended his ambitions to become mine host. There were whispers that somebody somewhere did not want him to succeed in the business world. No smoke without fire.

I was often given a lift from the Chadwell Heath training ground in Bobby's top of the range 4.2 litre Jaguar, and I reminded him of "the old days" when he used to drive around in his second-hand fire engine red Ford Zephyr. He was gathering wealth, but was the same old Bobby – cautious and controlled until loosened by a lager or three, and keeping everything close to his chest. Few ever knew exactly what was going on in Bobby's mind. As when playing, he would put up a defensive barrier.

His most disastrous business venture came when he was left holding most of the bills after an Essex country club he opened with several associates including Sean Connery went bust with huge debts. It all turned sour amid rumours of underworld attempts to burn down the club, and a shotgun shooting incident involving one of the partners. Bobby was shaken *and* stirred. But I am not judging Bobby Moore the businessman, only the footballer, and few defenders since the first ball was kicked have played the game so well. Football was a business in which he was second to none. He was the Great Defender.

CAP 48
Northern Ireland, Windsor Park, 22.10.66. England won 2-0
Banks   Cohen Wilson Stiles   Charlton J. Moore*
Ball   Hurst Charlton R.   Hunt[1] Peters[1]

Highlights: The Irish, with George Best and Derek Dougan in menacing mood, battled desperately to overcome England in their first match as world champions, but they were sunk by a goal in each half by first Roger Hunt and then Martin Peters. The match deteriorated into a bad tempered encounter, and in the closing minutes Linfield winger Billy Ferguson was ordered off after a savage tackle on Alan Ball. Bobby Moore's attention during the build up to the match was claimed by the Inland Revenue, who announced they would be taxing the £1,000 bonus collected by each of the 22 players in England's World Cup winning squad. On behalf of the team, skipper Bobby took the Taxman to the law courts and won a verdict that the payment should be tax-free. What a way to treat heroes.

> *BOBBY*: ❝We had the public on our side against the Inland Revenue. The Judge ruled that our bonus had 'the quality of an accolade' rather than employment income. All the players were in agreement that it was a disgrace that we had to go to court to get what we felt we had earned without the Taxman taking a cut. Against the Irish we got a taste of what it would be like as world champions. It made everybody play twice as hard against us to try to bring us down.❞

No 49
Czechoslovakia, Wembley, 2.11.66. Drew 0-0
Banks   Cohen Wilson Stiles   Charlton J. Moore*
Ball   Hurst Charlton R. Hunt Peters

Highlights: This was the sixteenth match since the summer of 1965 in which England had not conceded a goal. The Czechs came only to defend, and their nine-man blanket defence smothered the England attack. England were now unbeaten in their last eighteen matches, and losing only once in their last twenty-nine, but this was a below-par performance that disappointed the 75,000 crowd. For the record, it was only the second goalless draw in fifty-eight post-war full internationals at Wembley. The only other one was the World Cup curtain-raiser against Uruguay.

BOBBY: 'This was one of the most frustrating matches in which I played at Wembley. We were so keen to play like world champions in our first match back at the ground where we won the trophy, but the Czechs just came to spoil and smother. There was some jeering as we came off at the end. That really hurt, but I suppose we just had to accept that we were now being judged by the standards we had set in winning the World Cup.'

CAP 50
Wales, Wembley, 16.11.66. England won 5-1 (own goal[1])
Banks Cohen Wilson Stiles Charlton J.[1] Moore*
Ball Hurst[2] Charlton R.[1] Hunt Peters

Highlights: The Charlton brothers were both on the score-sheet and Geoff Hurst netted twice against a Welsh team that telegraphed their tactics by continually trying to play long balls to their twin strikers Wyn Davies and Ron Davies. Apart from a consolation headed goal by Wyn Davies, the England defence comfortably controlled the Welsh attack by shutting out their supply line from the wings. With both the Home Championship and qualification for the European championships at stake, the game had a hard competitive edge and the final scoreline flattered the world champions who were helped by an own goal from one of the hardest workers on the pitch, Terry Hennessey. Bobby Moore, playing in his fiftieth international, was exceptional in an England defence that was at its dominant best. This was to prove the last match in which the famous World Cup winning XI played together.

BOBBY: 'We had no idea this would be the last time we would play together. What we achieved was historic, and you could warm your hands on our team spirit. We were just like a club side. Putting five past a very strong Wales team was, I suppose, a good way for it to end.'

CAP 51
Scotland, Wembley, 15.4.67. England lost 3-2
Banks Cohen Wilson Stiles Charlton J.[1] Moore*
Ball Greaves Charlton R. Hurst[1] Peters

Highlights: Scotland claimed they were world champions after handing England their first defeat in twenty matches, but it was something of a hollow victory against a team reduced to eight fit players. Jack Charlton hobbled at centre-forward for much of the match with a broken toe, Ray Wilson was a limping passenger after getting a kick on the ankle, and Jimmy Greaves was reduced to half pace by a knock in his comeback match. Denis Law was at his tormenting best and gave Scotland the lead after twenty-eight minutes, and it remained at 1-0 until a four-goal rush in the last twelve minutes. Celtic winger Bobby Lennox made it 2-0 before the limping Jack Charlton bravely pulled one back. Gordon Banks was beaten at the near post by Jim McCalliog and then Hurst headed home a Bobby Charlton cross. Four of the Scottish team helped Celtic become the first British club to win the European Cup the following month. The newly knighted Sir Alf Ramsey said: 'Scotland deserved their victory, but I hope they will accept it as a fact rather than an excuse when I say were were heavily handicapped by injuries.'

BOBBY: ❝The Scots were really stoked up for this one, and they played as if it was *their* World Cup final. I'm not going to take anything away from them because they were good value for their win, but I am sure it would have been a different story if we'd not had three players reduced to passengers. The big talking point was how long would it be before substitutes were allowed in international matches now that they had been introduced at club level?❞

**EYEWITNESS
NOBBY
STILES**

We knew the Scots meant business when my Manchester United team-mate Denis Law came out wearing shinpads for the first time that I could remember. He was ready to run through brick walls. Denis had famously thrown his golf clubs when he heard England had won the World Cup. They claimed they were world champions after they had beaten us, not accepting that we were reduced to just eight fully fit players. In my opinion, Bobby Moore was a great captain and a great player. From the moment I got into the team he was always supportive and encouraging, and helped me believe in myself. He was the most composed player ever. No matter what mayhem was going on around him, he always remained cool and in control. Most of us would come off at the end looking like wet rags, but Bobby would be immaculate, yet he would have put in a full shift. He was always as cool as a cucumber.

CAP 52
Spain, Wembley, 24.5.67. England won 2-0

Bonetti Cohen Newton Mullery   Labone   Moore*
Ball Greaves[1] Hurst Hunt[1] Hollins

Highlights: John Hollins won his only cap for England and played a prominent part in the first goal. His centre to the far post was headed down by Alan Ball into the path of Roger Hunt, whose shot was blocked and Jimmy Greaves banged in the rebound. It was his forty-fourth and final goal for England in his 57th international appearance. Hunt scored England's second goal in a match played for much of the time in a torrential downpour. Peter Bonetti, Keith Newton, Brian Labone and John Hollins were all brought into the Ramsey fold as he started to build for the 1968 European championship finals.

> *BOBBY*: 'Greavsie was the greatest English goal scorer of my time in the game, and long before it too! He could make something out of nothing, a real magician with the ball at his feet. We all felt sorry for him that he missed out on the World Cup final. He remained a great mate of mine, and we had memorable times together on and off the pitch.'

CAP 53
Austria, Vienna, 27.5.67. England won 1-0

Bonetti Newton Wilson   Mullery Labone Moore*
Ball[1]   Greaves Hurst Hunt Hunter

Highlights: This was Sir Alf Ramsey's fiftieth match since he took over and his thirty-third victory. It was also a milestone match for Harold Shepherdson, who was on the touchline for his hundredth match as England trainer. A neatly worked goal by Alan Ball in the twentieth minute won the match. The England squad then went off on a trip to Canada thinly disguised as an FA XI as part of the Expo 67 festivities. The nadir of a pointless exercise was Sir Alf getting caught up in a heated argument over the state of the pitch in Montreal which had been used for a circus parade a day before the game.

> *BOBBY*: 'In one of the great unexpected and original quotes from any football manager, Sir Alf fumed in his clipped tones: 'I will not allow my players to risk injury on a disgraceful pitch that is covered in elephant shit.' I had rarely seen Alf as angry, apart of course from the quarter-final against Argentina!'

CAP 54
Wales, Ninian Park, 21.10.67. England won 3-0
Banks Cohen Newton Mullery Charlton J.   Moore*
Ball[1] Hunt   Charlton R.[1] Hurst Peters[1]

Highlights: The match turned on a magnificent save by Gordon Banks. Wales were having the better of the early play in a rainstorm when his Stoke team-mate Roy Vernon fired a shot from point-blank range. Somehow Banks managed to fist the ball off target, and from then on England took command. Martin Peters and Bobby Charlton scored a goal each and Alan Ball netted from the penalty spot. Mike England stood like a man mountain in the middle of the Welsh defence, and gave added ammunition to his Tottenham supporters who claimed with some justification that he was the best centre-half in Britain.

> *BOBBY*: ❛Gordon made many incredible saves, but this one really stood out. I was resigned to a goal when Roy Vernon took aim from just a few yards. He was one of the most clinical finishers in the League, and there was no way he could miss from there. But Gordon came from nowhere to punch the ball away. Roy couldn't believe it, nor could the Welsh fans who were celebrating a goal and neither could I. It really lifted the team and we went on to a comfortable victory. Banksie was the king of goalkeepers.❜

CAP 55
Northern Ireland, Wembley, 22.11.67. England won 2-0
Banks   Cohen Wilson Mullery Sadler   Moore*
Thompson Hunt   Charlton R.[1] Hurst[1]   Peters

Highlights: Versatile David Sadler made his debut at centre-half against a Northern Ireland team missing their two key forwards George Best and Derek Dougan. Goals from Geoff Hurst and Bobby Charlton clinched victory in an undistinguished match that fell flat the moment it was announced just before the kick-off that both Best and Dougan had failed fitness tests.

> *BOBBY*: ❛This was a dull game but an important victory. All attention was now switched to the final Home Championship match against Scotland that would decide which of us would represent Great Britain in the European Nations Cup quarter finals. Once the Doog and Best pulled out, we knew our job was going to be much easier. George in particular could win matches on his own.❜

CAP 56

USSR, Wembley, 6.12.67. Drew 2-2

Banks Knowles Wilson Mullery Sadler Moore*

Ball[1] Hunt Charlton R. Hurst Peters[1]

Highlights: Ray Wilson was given a rare chasing on a snow-carpeted pitch by flying Russian winger Chislenko, who appropriately was also an outstanding ice hockey player. Alan Ball gave England an early lead, but two goals from 'Red Rocket' Chislenko put Russia in command. Bobby Moore and Ray Wilson combined to make an opening for Martin Peters, who headed an equaliser. Tottenham defender Cyril Knowles made an assured debut out of position at right-back. Pshenichnikov proved himself a worthy successor to Lev Yashin in goal with a series of stunning saves as England pressed for victory in the last twenty minutes of a skilled and entertaining match that was a credit to both sides.

> *BOBBY*: 'I had never known Wembley's surface so challenging. You needed ice-skates rather than football boots, and poor old Ray had a nightmare trying to mark Chislenko. It would have been hard enough on the usual Wembley turf, but turning on the icy top meant you easily lost your footing. Alf summed it up afterwards when he said, 'That's best forgotten.''

CAP 57

Scotland, Hampden Park, 24.2.68. Drew 1-1

Banks Newton Wilson Mullery Labone Moore*

Ball Hurst Summerbee Charlton R. Peters[1]

Highlights: England needed a draw to qualify for the European championship quarter-finals, Scotland a win. Martin Peters produced one of his most impressive performances for England, scoring their goal with a superbly controlled swerving shot and going close on three other occasions. John Hughes headed Scotland's equaliser when Gordon Banks slipped on the treacherous surface that was a mixture of mud and ice. Charlie Cooke had a brilliant twenty-minute spell when he ran the England defence dizzy, but the Scottish strikers could not cash in on his creative work. Mike Summerbee made a quietly impressive debut.

> *BOBBY*: 'Sir Alf famously described Martin Peters as ten years ahead of his time, and you could see what he meant in this game. He was a thought and a move ahead of everybody on the pitch and kept popping up in unexpected places, completely deceiving the Scottish defenders.'

CAP 58
Spain, Wembley, 3.4.68. England won 1-0
Banks Knowles Wilson Mullery Charlton J. Moore*
Ball Hunt Summerbee Charlton R.[1] Peters

Highlights: Bobby Charlton crashed the ball into the net from a short free-kick taken by Martin Peters to equal the 44-goal England record held by Jimmy Greaves. Spain threatened to snatch a last minute equaliser in this first leg European championship quarter-final tie, but Banks pulled off a spectacular save from a lightning back heel by Amancio. The Spaniards played a cautious defensive game, putting their faith in a victory in the second leg in Madrid.

BOBBY: ❛Bobby Charlton had been banging the ball into the net for England as long as I had been in the game, and this was yet another of his specials that gave us a vital lead to take into the second leg. Spain came only to defend and we knew it was going to be much tougher in Madrid.❜

CAP 59
Spain, Madrid, 8.5.68. England won 2-1
Bonetti Newton Wilson Mullery   Labone Moore*
Ball Peters[1] Charlton R. Hunt Hunter[1]

Highlights: When Geoff Hurst pulled out of this European championship quarter-final second leg at the last minute with a damaged toe, Sir Alf Ramey juggled his team and summoned Norman 'Bites Yer Legs' Hunter as an extra containing player. Amancio brought the scores level on aggregate in the first minute of the second-half of a match played with a fierce determination. Martin Peters quickly restored England's advantage when he headed in an Alan Ball corner. Ten minutes from the end Roger Hunt collected an Alan Mullery throw, and his cross was thrashed into the net by, of all people, Hunter, scoring a rare goal with one of the most under-used right boots in football.

BOBBY: ❛This victory clinched our place in the European championship semi-finals in Italy. I'm not sure who was more surprised by Hunter's goal, the Spanish goalkeeper or Norman himself. I couldn't remember the last time I'd seen him kick the ball with his right foot, let alone score with it. It was one of the few times I laughed out loud at an England goal. Our confidence was back as high as when we won the World Cup in 1966 and we looked forward to trying to add the European title to the Jules Rimet trophy.❜

Bobby's long-time understudy Norman 'Bites Yer Legs' Hunter on the prowl

CAP 60
Sweden, Wembley, 22.5.68. England won 3-1

Stepney Newton Knowles Mullery Labone Moore*
Ball Peters[1] Charlton R.[1] (Hurst) Hunt[1] Hunter

Highlights: Alex Stepney played his only game in the England goal one week before helping Manchester United win the European Cup on the same pitch. Colin Bell also made his first appearance, and inspired goals from Peters, Hunt and a classic from Charlton, who became the new record holder with forty-five goals before limping off to be replaced by Geoff Hurst. Charlton recovered from his injury to lead United to their emotional European Cup victory over Benfica. There was a worrying climax to the game when Swedish goalkeeper Larsson was carried off with a fractured skull after he had bravely dived at the feet of Alan Mullery.

> *BOBBY*: "We held our breath when Bobby Charlton limped off with the European Cup final so close, but thank goodness he was fit enough to lead United to their amazing victory over Benfica. I cried the day of the Munich air crash in 1958, and was willing United to win the trophy in memory of all those who died, including my hero Duncan Edwards."

CAP 61
West Germany, Hanover, 1.6.68. England lost 1-0

Banks Newton Knowles Hunter Labone Moore*
Ball Bell Summerbee Hurst Thompson

Highlights: England's unbeaten record against the Germans, which had lasted twelve matches and sixty-seven years, ended when Brian Labone deflected a Franz Beckenbauer shot wide of Gordon Banks eight minutes from the end. It was a goal that silenced the jeers of the German spectators who had been barracking their own team as England made and missed a string of chances.

> *BOBBY*: "We should have had the game stitched up long before Franz scored with a shot that got a wicked deflection. This was only our third defeat in our last forty matches, and we headed for the European Nations Cup semi-final against Yugoslavia in Florence in good spirit."

Coming up, one of the most brutal matches in which England played throughout Bobby's 108-match international career.

ENGLAND were proud world champions when Bobby led them into the 1968 European Nations Cup, soon to be renamed the European Football Championship. By the time the finals were over, England's pride had been severely bruised and dented and the game as we knew it was to change forever. If you could be transported back to that period you would see football unrecognisable from today's more sanitised and softer game. This was one of the last tournaments in which the boot ruled, and scything tackles were a physical part and parcel of the proceedings.

The semi-final against Yugoslavia was staged in Florence, the cultural heart of Tuscany, but what we witnessed was not so much da Vinci as da violence.

They kicked lumps out of each other. Through English eyes it looked as if the Yugoslavs were the authors of the conflict, but neutrals could see that England were also putting it about in response to some vicious tackling. Later, the Yuoslavs were to claim with some justification that Norman Hunter had started it all when his ferocious early tackle left their chief schemer Osmin a limping passenger. From then on every Yugoslav challenge was laced with menace.

You would never see a game like this today. There would be more red cards than Paul Daniels has ever flashed. The maestro Bobby Moore managed to stay aloof.

CAP 62
Yugoslavia, Florence, 5.6.68. England lost 1-0
Banks Newton Wilson Mullery Labone   Moore*
Ball   Peters   Charlton R.   Hunt   Hunter

Highlights: It was fitting that the only goal of the match was scored by the best player on the pitch, Dragan 'Magic' Dzajic, who would have been a certainty for the Premier League today. He was like George Best and Jimmy Greaves rolled into one, quick, clever and decisive. Bobby Moore made one of his rare errors that could be counted on the fingers of a one-arm bandit. He failed with an attempted headed clearance that left the ball as a gift for Dzajic, who swiftly steered it wide of the stranded Gordon Banks. There were just five minutes left for England to save their Euro championship lives, and (Mr Mainwaring) there was panic in the ranks. Alan Mullery became enveloped in a red mist, and – after being hacked for the umpteenth time – retaliated with a deliberate kick in the unmentionables of an annoying wasp of a player called Dobrivoje Trivic. It is probably being written for the thousandth time that this brought Mullery the ignominy of being the first England player ever sent off. I often see it reported that he was red carded, but it was two years and the World Cup in Mexico before the card system dreamt up by English referee Ken Aston was introduced in international football. He was sent packing with the good old-fashioned pointed finger. In many ways the 1968 European championships were a turning point for football. The powers-that-be at Fifa were determined to make the game less physical. If you could sit down and watch a full replay of the Yugoslavia/England match you would understand why many thought the game had become too much of a physical challenge, with skill being forced to take second place to strength.

BOBBY: ❝I have to own up to being responsible for their goal. I misjudged my timing when trying to head clear a ball floated into the penalty area, and missed it completely. The brilliant Dzajic was not going to miss a gift like that. It was a really nasty game, and I could sympathise with Mullers when he angrily retaliated after yet again being kicked from behind.❞

**EYEWITNESS
ALAN
MULLERY**

When the referee ordered me off it was the worst moment of my career. I felt as if I had not only let the team down but also my wife and family. The Yugoslav player I kicked out at had been hacking at me throughout the game and I just lost my temper. That was unprofessional of me and I have never forgiven myself. To be the first England player ever sent off is a record I will hate having to live with. If I could turn the clock back I would control my temper. Bobby showed me great sympathy, and was a witness of the stick I'd taken throughout the game. He was a giant of a player. The bigger the stage, the better he performed. It was a privilege to play with him at Fulham at the back end of his career. He was an absolute master of the defensive arts, a great role model and a smashing bloke who did not have a shred of arrogance. He is an easy choice when selecting all-time great teams.

CAP 63

USSR, Rome, 8.6.68. England won 2-0

Banks Wright Wilson Stiles Labone Moore*
Hunter Hunt Charlton R.[1] Hurst[1] Peters

Highlights: Goals from Bobby Charlton and Geoff Hurst lifted England to victory in this play-off for third place in the European championship finals. Nobby Stiles was recalled for his first England match for fourteen months in place of the suspended Alan Mullery, and played in his trademark tigerish style. The Russians had been deadlocked with Italy after extra-time in a goalless semi-final. Italy went through to the final on an unsatisfactory toss of a coin. Italy then beat Yugoslavia 2-0 in a replay of the final after a 1-1 draw. For Sir Alf Ramsey and his England players the priority now was the defence of their World Cup in Mexico in 1970.

BOBBY: ❝Our victory over the Russians was some consolation, but we'd gone to Italy to win the European championship trophy and so we considered our trip a flop. The Russians were flat after losing their semi-final on the farcical toss of a coin. There was a storm of criticism over the method for deciding a deadlocked match, and it hurried the introduction of penalty shoot-outs.❞

CAP 64

Romania, Bucharest, 6.11.68. Drew 0-0

Banks Wright (McNab) Newton Mullery Labone Moore*
Ball Hunt Charlton R. Hurst Peters

Highlights: Tommy Wright, who had partnered his Everton team-mate Ray Wilson at full-back against Russia, now had Blackburn's Keith Newton playing with him at left-back. England's World Cup heroes Cohen and Wilson had both had their international careers ended by injuries after playing together in twenty-seven matches. Wright and Newton, who would later continue their partnership at club level with Everton, hardly had time to get to know each other before Wright went off injured in the tenth minute to be replaced by Arsenal's Bob McNab who, despite playing out of position, gave a sound debut performance in a dreary, defence-dominated match.

BOBBY: ❝Alf was now building a team with the 1970 World Cup defence in mind, and his first priority was finding defenders to replace George and Ray, arguably the best full-back partnership England had ever had. They played a huge part in our World Cup success.❞

CAP 65
Bulgaria, Wembley, 11.12.68. Drew 1-1

West Newton (Reaney) McNab Mullery Labone Moore*
Lee Bell Charlton R. Hurst[1] Peters

Highlights: Francis Lee made his first England appearance alongside his Manchester City team-mate Colin Bell, and his thrusting runs down the right wing were a continual source of danger to a packed Bulgarian defence. There were also first England caps for goalkeeper Gordon West and Leeds full-back Paul Reaney, who came on as a substitute for injured Keith Newton. Geoff Hurst scored England's goal, and the Bulgarians replied with a magnificent solo goal by powerful centre-forward Asparuhov.

> *BOBBY*: ❛Francis Lee and Colin Bell brought their Manchester City pace and precision to the team, and it made me realise we were suddenly under the influence of my old mate and teacher Malcolm Allison. It was difficult for them to make a good impression because Bulgaria packed their defence and just wanted to avoid defeat, but Franny still managed to make a good impression in his debut.❜

Romania, Wembley, 15.1.69. Drew 1-1

Banks Wright McNab Stiles Charlton J.[1] Hunter
Radford Hunt Charlton R.* Hurst Ball

Highlights: A memorable match for the Charlton brothers. Bobby captained the team in injured Bobby Moore's absence in what was his ninetieth international, and big Jack scored England's goal. It was John Radford's first game for England and Roger Hunt's last. Hunt was sick of the criticism being aimed at him during an unsuccessful press campaign to get Jimmy Greaves recalled, and he asked Ramsey not to consider him for any more matches.

CAP 66
France, Wembley, 12.3.69. England won 5-0

Banks Newton Cooper Mullery Charlton J. Moore*
Lee[1] Bell Hurst[3] Peters O'Grady[1]

Highlights: Geoff Hurst was again a hat-trick hero, this time two of his goals against an outclassed French side coming from the penalty spot. Francis Lee scored his first goal for England and Mike O'Grady, recalled after six years in the wilderness, was also on the mark. Terry Cooper was Keith Newton's new left-back partner as Ramsey continued his search for a duo to compare with Cohen and Wilson. It was a relief for Sir Alf to find his forwards on the mark after only four goals in the previous six internationals. There were two Wembley milestones. This was England's 100th victory against overseas opponents, and Hurst's goal was the 200th by England at the twin-towered cathedral of English football.

> *BOBBY*: 'Alf had been under great pressure to recall Jimmy Greaves, and he told the press. 'I'm being crucified because I am not picking Jimmy. People need to know he has asked me not to select him.' Greavsie had told Alf he did not want to be considered for the squad if he was not going to play. Alf took that to mean he did not want to play for England. It was all a misunderstanding, and Jimmy never got to play for his country again. England's loss.'

CAP 67
Northern Ireland, Windsor Park, 3.5.69. England won 3-1
Banks Newton McNab Mullery Labone Moore*
Ball Lee[1] Charlton R. Hurst[1] Peters[1]

Highlights: The scoreline flattered England. Goalkeeper Gordon Banks was under long periods of pressure after Eric McMordie had cancelled out an early Martin Peters goal. With Newton doing an excellent containing job on George Best, England began to gain command. Goals from Francis Lee and Geoff Hurst wrapped up the game for them but not before Banks had made two splendid saves against the always dangerous Derek Dougan. Live television cut the attendance to 23,000.

> *BOBBY*: 'Alf was greatly impressed by Keith Newton's performance against George Best. Keith marked him as well as I had ever seen, and kept the Irish genius as quiet as it was possible. I know Alf had decided he had found his right-back replacement for George Cohen.'

CAPS 68
Wales, Wembley, 7.5.69. England won 2-1
West Newton Cooper Moore* Charlton J. Hunter
Lee[1] Bell Astle Charlton R.[1] Ball

Highlights: Wyn Davies gave Wales the lead and they were looking the better team when England were awarded a penalty that Francis Lee fired against the woodwork. The miss seemed to inspire rather than depress the Manchester City striker, and he laid on the equaliser for Bobby Charlton following a smart exchange of wall passes. Lee then notched the winner after a drive from lively debutant Jeff Astle had been cleared off the line.

BOBBY: ❛I was selected at right-half with Norman Hunter taking the No 6 shirt, playing alongside his Leeds team-mate Jack Charlton. I was happy to do whatever Alf wanted, but I was always more comfortable when with our backs to goal being on the left of the centre-half, particularly when my West Ham clubmates Geoff and Martin were in the team. I could find them with the ball almost with my eyes closed.❜

CAP 69
Scotland, Wembley, 10.5.69. England won 4-1
Banks Newton Cooper Mullery Labone Moore*
Lee Ball Charlton R. Hurst[2] Peters[2]

Highlights: The old West Ham double act of Hurst and Peters sank the Scots with two goals each, the second of Hurst's goals coming from a thunderous penalty that many observers considered the hardest they had ever seen a ball hit from the spot. Colin Stein scored to make it 2-1 at half-time, and the final scoreline was harsh on a Scottish team powerfully driven from midfield by Billy Bremner and Archie Gemmill. The victory put England in just the right mood for their fact-finding tour in preparation for their 1970 World Cup defence.

BOBBY: ❛Alf was always extra keen to beat the Scots, and he gave an indication of the way he was thinking for the defence of the World Cup. He selected what he considered his strongest team for this match against the 'Auld Enemy'. He was delighted with our overwhelming victory and in a rare loose moment over his favourite tipple of a gin and tonic said, 'I think we have a team as good as the 1966 side.'❜

CAP 70
Mexico, Ciudad de México, 1.6.69. Drew 0-0
West Newton (Wright) Cooper Mullery Labone Moore*
Lee Ball Charlton R. Hurst Peters

Highlights: Goalkeeper Gordon West played impressively as deputy for Gordon Banks, and then astonished Ramsey by asking not to be considered for any more internationals because he suffered so much from homesickness. The England team

Bobby flanked by Martin Peters and Geoff Hurst, the Three Musketeers of England and West Ham

struggled in the second-half as Mexico's high altitude took its toll, and Ramsey noted that he would need to give them several weeks to acclimatise before the 1970 World Cup finals. An unofficial international followed three days later in which an FA XI won 4-0 as Sir Alf gave every player in his squad experience of action in the thin air of Mexico.

> *BOBBY*: ❝Playing for just an hour in Mexico made you feel as if your lungs were going to burst, and to go the full ninety minutes was exhausting. It was obvious we would need more time to acclimatise to the high altitude when we were back defending the World Cup. Alf accepted this and started making plans for our return the following year.❞

CAP 71
Uruguay, Montevideo, 8.6.69. England won 2-1
Banks Wright Newton Mullery Labone Moore*
Lee[1] Bell Hurst[1] Ball Peters

Highlights: Gordon Banks, back in the England goal following a round-trip home to the UK for the funeral of his father, had to be at his best to keep out the Uruguay attack after Francis Lee had scored an early goal. Banks was beaten by a diving header from the exceptional Luis Cubilla, before Hurst collected the winner ten minutes from the end following neat approach work by Ball and Lee. The game was played in the Centenario Stadium, the venue for the first World Cup final in 1930.

> *BOBBY*: ❝We were in awe of Banksie. He played out of his skin. It was a superhuman display considering he had flown back to England for his Dad's funeral and then rejoined us in time to play against a very talented Uruguayan team. It filled all of us with confidence when we looked back to see him on the goal-line.❞

CAP 72
Brazil, Rio de Janeiro, 12.6.69. England lost 2-1
Banks Wright Newton Mullery Labone Moore*
Ball Bell[1] Charlton R. Hurst Peters

Highlights: Colin Bell gave England a 1-0 half-time lead and victory hopes were high when Banks saved a penalty from Brazilian skipper Carlos Alberto that briefly silenced the 160,000 crowd in the magnificent Maracana Stadium. Alan Mullery policed Pele so well that he made hardly any impact on the match, but England tired in the final twenty minutes and they were brought to their knees by late goals from Tostao and Jairzinho. Sir Alf Ramsey said after the match: 'I am proud of every one of my players. We were so close to a deserved victory. I am delighted with our overall performances on this tour, and it will be of great benefit when we come back next year for the World Cup.'

> *BOBBY*: ❛That was as well as we had played against Brazil, and we deserved to come away with at least a draw. In the end we were beaten by tiredness after an exhausting tour. Mullers did a fantastic marking job on Pele, who hardly made any impact. It's not often you say that!❜

CAP 73
Holland, Amsterdam, 5.11.69. England won 1-0
Bonetti Wright Hughes Mullery   Charlton J. Moore*
Lee (Thompson) Bell[1] Charlton R. Hurst Peters

Highlights: Colin Bell scored the goal that defeated a Dutch team that played the more skilful football but without being able to provide the finishing touch to their impressive approach work. Emlyn Hughes made a sound start to his England career at left-back. It was Guy Fawkes Day, but there were few fireworks from an England attack that too often put passes astray. The game was into its last five minutes when Bell netted the winning goal following a mishit shot by Bobby Charlton. It was deserved reward for an all-action display from Bell, who had earlier put a header against the bar. His energetic performance showed why his Manchester City coach Malcolm Allison had nicknamed him Nijinsky (after the race horse, not the ballet master).

> *BOBBY*: ❛The talk among we England players after the match was the performance of young Ajax partners Rudi Krol and Johan Cruyff. We all knew we would be hearing a lot more about them. They were so comfortable on the ball and oozed class.❜

CAP 74
Portugal, Wembley, 10.12.69. England won 1-0
Bonetti Reaney Hughes Mullery   Charlton J.[1]   Moore*
Lee   Bell (Peters) Astle   Charlton R. Ball

Highlights: Francis Lee, noted as one of the deadliest of all penalty takers, missed his second spot-kick in an England shirt. England were awarded the penalty after Jeff Astle had been brought down. Lee stumbled as he ran up to take the kick and sliced the ball so wide it nearly hit a corner flag. It took centre-half Jack Charlton to show the forwards how to get the ball into the net on a pitch made heavy by incessant rain. Jack rose high to head in a corner from brother Bobby in the twenty-fourth minute of an undistinguished match. Martin Peters was summoned on as second-half substitute for Colin Bell, who went off with a dislocated shoulder.

BOBBY: ❛It was a shock to see Franny Lee making such a mess of a penalty. He became a legend at Manchester City for his spot-kicks and earned the nickname Lee Won Pen. He lost his footing on the terrible surface, and missed by a mile. He was the most relieved player on the pitch when the Charlton brothers combined for the winning goal.❜

Holland, Wembley, 14.1.70. Drew 0-0
Banks Newton Cooper Peters   Charlton J. Hunter
Lee (Mullery) Bell Jones (Hurst) Charlton R.*   Storey-Moore

Highlights: England, missing injured Bobby Moore, were jeered by their fans who did not appreciate that Holland were an emerging power in world football. The Dutch team included such quality players as Cruyff, Van Hanegem, Krol and Keizer, and England's defenders had to work flat out to hold them. Mick Jones, playing his first international match for four years, was substituted by Geoff Hurst after seventy minutes. Ian Storey-Moore, making his one and only England appearance, had a good-looking headed goal disallowed. The referee blew the final whistle as Bobby Charlton unleashed one of his specials that flew into the net, but too late to count. It was another milestone match for Bobby, who in his ninety-eighth international overtook the Billy Wright record of sixty-seven matches against overseas opposition.

CAP 75
Belgium, Brussels, 25.2.70. England won 3-1
Banks Wright Cooper Moore* Labone   Hughes
Lee   Ball[2] Osgood Hurst[1] Peters

Highlights: Alan Ball was rewarded for one of his typically non-stop performances with two goals in appalling conditions in rain-lashed Brussels. Geoff Hurst scored the other goal against a punchless Belgium team which had Paul van Himst as their one world-class player. Chelsea's graceful but unpredictable Peter Osgood made a quietly satisfactory debut on a pitch that made ball control a challenge. The game was won by England in midfield, where Ball and Peters were outstanding and always a thought and a deed ahead of their Belgian markers.

BOBBY: ❝The conditions were so bad that the game was in danger of being abandoned. The lashing sleet and rain got into our eyes and made it difficult to see the ball, let alone control it. Yet Ballie and Martin managed to turn the Belgian defence inside out with their passing and positioning. They were both fantastic. ❞

CAP 76
Wales, Ninian Park, 18.4.70. Drew 1-1
Banks   Wright   Hughes   Mullery   Labone   Moore*
Lee[1]   Ball   Charlton R.   Hurst   Peters

Highlights: Sir Alf Ramsey was shaping his tactics for the coming defence of the World Cup, and had decided on a 4-4-2 formation with Francis Lee and Geoff Hurst as the two front runners supported from midfield by Alan Mullery, Alan Ball, Bobby Charlton and Martin Peters. There was press criticism of the system after England had struggled to hold Wales, Lee salvaging a draw with a spectacular solo goal after Dick Krzywicki had given the Welsh a well-deserved lead. Sir Alf said later that he was satisfied with the performance. 'Everything we do now is with Mexico in mind,' he said. 'We must adapt the way we play for the conditions we will meet out there.'

BOBBY: ❝Alf had been experimenting for months with different formations, and following our summer tour experience in Mexico had settled for 4-4-2. It was pointless trying to judge the system needed for the high altitude of Mexico by the conditions in Cardiff. It was obvious we were going to need to conserve our energy in the thin air, and 4-4-2 meant our midfielders would get and give more support. ❞

CAP 77
Northern Ireland, Wembley, 21.4.70. England won 3-1
Banks   Newton (Bell)   Hughes   Mullery   Moore*   Stiles
Coates   Kidd   Charlton R.[1]   Hurst[1]   Peters[1]

Highlights: Bobby Charlton led the team out in his 100th appearance in an England shirt and celebrated with his 48th goal. Peters, now of Tottenham, and Hurst were also on the mark to give England a comfortable victory. George Best gave Northern Ireland a rare moment of supremacy when he took advantage of dithering in the England defence to turn a half chance into a goal. Ralph Coates and Brian Kidd made their debuts as Ramsey searched for his ideal combination for the World Cup finals.

BOBBY: ❛There were six of the team who had won the World Cup in this match against the Irish, and Ballie and Jack Charlton were still in the squad. This underlined Alf's loyalty. Only George Cohen, Ray Wilson and Roger Hunt would not be making the trip to Mexico.❜

CAP 78
Scotland, Hampden Park, 25.4.70. Drew 0-0
Banks Newton Hughes Stiles Labone Moore*
Thompson (Mullery) Ball Astle   Hurst   Peters

Highlights: This was England's final game before flying off for the World Cup warm-up games in South America, and the Scots were hell bent on giving them a morale-sapping defeat as a farewell present. England were equally determined not to be beaten and the game became bogged down in a midfield stalemate. A buffeting wind whipped around Hampden and made ball control difficult, robbing the 137,438 spectators of what had been an anticipated classic.

BOBBY: ❛Remarkably, this game produced the first goalless draw between Scotland and England since the first ever international football match between us back in 1872. The Scots did their best to knock our confidence, but we would not give them an inch. The wind was so strong it threatened to blow us off our feet, and the match was one long slog. Not a pretty sight.❜

The Bobby Moore adventure was now about to enter the world of the surreal, sinister, farcical and frightening. A Hollywood screenwriter with an over-heated imagination could not have made it up.

Every English football fan would find out how to discover Bogota on the world map.

Chapter 12: The Bogota Boobytrap

EVEN now – more than forty years since Bobby Moore was arrested in Bogota, accused of stealing a bracelet from a hotel jewellery shop in the Colombian capital – I am often asked with a whisper and a wink, "Come on, tell us ... did Bobby nick that bracelet?"

Of course he didn't, and it was long ago proved that he was the victim of an attempted sting, but it is human nature that people like to think the worst. I found out within 48 hours of Bobby's arrest that he had almost certainly been framed, but it was years before he was officially cleared. I was in Mexico City at the time and at the insistence of my London editor Derek Marks went to every embassy, where I was repeatedly told that Bogota was notorious for this sort of con. There were a string of complaints from tourists on record at each embassy, and an aide to the American ambassador told me: "We call it the Bogota boobytrap."

That inspired the headline they put on my front page lead story filed to the *Daily Express:* "BOBBY CAUGHT IN THE BOGOTA BOOBYTRAP."

It was a nonsense to even suspect Bobby of the crime. As his closest pal Jimmy Greaves said on hearing the news when he arrived in Mexico City at the end of his World Cup rally drive: "Bobby's nicked a bracelet? Why? He could afford to buy the bloody shop." Only he didn't say bloody.

Colombian police papers released in 2003 – ten years after Bobby's passing and thirty years after the fiasco – finally revealed that they had believed all along that he was innocent. He had never taken the shop owners on in a legal battle because he feared false evidence being produced.

BOBBY: ❛I went through hell, but never let on how it was affecting me. The only thing that mattered is that I knew I was innocent. Bobby Charlton was with me in the shop and he also knew I was innocent. They were trying to stitch me up, and I was determined not to let them know they had me concerned in any way. My house arrest in Bogota was as farcical as everything else, and the two guards they assigned to me could have stepped out of a Laurel and Hardy film. It was one of those crazy situations where you didn't know whether to laugh or cry. I trained my thoughts on only one thing, getting back to the England squad and playing in the World Cup.❜

An interlude here to lighten the mood, and it is a story with which I made Bobby laugh out loud. It revolves around the late, much mourned Vic Railton, who was a mutual mate of both Bobby and me from way back. In 1970 he was making one of his rare trips abroad for the London *Evening News*. Vic was the best contacts man in the business, but very much an office-bound reporter. He did it all by telephone, and the likes of Ron Greenwood, Bill Nicholson, Tommy Docherty and Billy Wright would call him back if ever he left a message. He won their trust by never breaking confidences and would always keep them informed with the latest hot football gossip.

Vic's empire was his office in the days when the *News* was based at Carmelite House, off Fleet Street. While he had his bank of telephones and giant contacts book, he was safe and in control. But once outside, he was like a barracuda out of water. And as for going abroad, he hated it. For Vic, north of Watford was foreign land.

Very reluctantly, he joined the England team on their build-up tour leading to the 1970 finals in Mexico. The man with a nose for news at home was never comfortable on trips away from home, and he considered flying was strictly for the birds.

He showed he had lost all news reporting sense when he boarded the plane with the England team at Bogota for the final lap to Mexico, a flight already heavy with the despair of the six players who were out of the 28-man squad. The pilot was just bringing up the wheels when Vic shared a secret with the rest of the press party. "Here," he said. "Three guesses as to who's not on the plane …"

It was the day Bobby Moore had been arrested at the airport on the trumped-up jewel-theft charge.

Fifteen reporters were trying to decide whether to strangle Vic or hijack the plane and make the pilot head back to Colombia. The *Daily Mail's* enterprising Ron Crowther (a brilliant reporter beautifully nicknamed Ron Von Ruintrip because of his constant grumbling) got the last seat on a plane from Mexico back to Bogota and was first to track down where Bobby was under house arrest.

Excited *Mail* editors gathered around the Telex machine for his exclusive story. This was the first copy they received: "Ron Crowther here in Bogota. What is the Spanish equivalent for shirt neck size fifteen and a half …?"

Another of my favourite anecdotes from that Mexican adventure involves the unique Geoffrey Green, legendary 'Association Football Correspondent' for *The Times* and Bobby's favourite character in our village world of football and the media

When Bobby Moore arrived in Mexico to rejoin the England squad after his five days under arrest in Colombia, I was among a posse of press reporters and photographers gathered on the tarmac of Mexico City airport to meet him (can you imagine the press being allowed on the tarmac in today's security-obsessed world?).

Prominent among us was the elegant, Peter O'Toole lookalike Green, arguably the greatest football writer of any time.

Geoffrey had a habit of using lines from songs when he talked, and he always greeted people with such phrases as "Younger than Springtime, baby", delivered in a cut-glass Oxbridge accent. He was using the phrase "I'm over the Moon" long before it became the cliché crutch of tongue-tied footballers.

As Bobby Moore stepped out from the plane into the dazzling, dancing light of scores of flashbulbs, he spotted the tall, willowy figure of Geoffrey among the hordes at the bottom of the steps.

He punched the air and shouted, "Over the rainbow, baby." Foreign reporters, anxious to record Bobby's first words on his return to freedom, scratched their heads as they tried to decipher what the England captain had said.

Back to the Bobby Moore football story ...

CAP 79
Colombia, Bogota, 20.5.70. England won 4-0
Banks Newton Cooper Mullery Labone   Moore*
Lee   Ball[1] Charlton R.[1]   Hurst   Peters[2]

Highlights: England arrived in Bogota after two weeks altitude training in Mexico. Sir Alf Ramsey fielded what he considered his number one World Cup team and two goals from Martin Peters and one each from Bobby Charlton and Alan Ball gave England a comfortable victory at an altitude of 8,600 feet high up in the spectacular Andes mountains. England were a goal up in just ninety seconds from a deft header by Peters, and were rarely troubled by a Colombian side that played a neat passing game but without penalty area punch. This 4-4-2 line-up featured Francis Lee and Geoff Hurst working in tandem up front and supported by a midfield quartet of Alan Mullery, Alan Ball, Bobby Charlton and Martin Peters. Everton skipper Brian Labone had taken over from Jack Charlton at the heart of the defence, and only Gordon Banks and Bobby Moore had survived from the fortress that had been so impressive in the 1966 World Cup finals. Nobby Stiles also made the trip, almost as Alf's lucky mascot.

BOBBY: ❛Alf and his backroom team – and in particular the team medical officer, Dr Neil Phillips – had got our preparations just right. We had learned from our summer tour in 1969 that we needed more time to get acclimatised, and the two weeks we spent in Mexico got us nicely adjusted to the thin air. It was two days before we cruised to this comfortable win over Colombia in Bogota that I casually went into the hotel jewellery shop with Bobby Charlton. He was looking for a present for his wife, Norma, and I went in with him just to pass the time. That was when the accusation was first made that I'd stolen the bracelet, but after I had strongly denied it I thought the matter had been dropped.❜

EYEWITNESS BOBBY CHARLTON

The whole thing was a farce from beginning to end. Bobby and I had no idea what they were on about when the accusation of a theft was first made, and we offered to be searched on the spot. But they didn't bother, and we thought that was the end of what had been a misunderstanding. I really admired Bobby for the way he took it all in his stride. I'm sure other players would have cracked and been unable to concentrate on their football, but he just rose above it all and had an outstanding tournament.

CAP 80
Ecuador, Quito, 24.5.70. England won 2-0
Banks Newton Cooper Mullery Labone   Moore*
Lee[1] (Kidd[1]) Ball Charlton R. (Sadler) Hurst Peters

Highlights: England literally went up into the clouds for this final warm-up match before the start of their World Cup defence. Quito is more than 9,000 feet above sea level, and the ball swerved around like a boomerang. Francis Lee gave England the lead and was then substituted in the seventieth minute by Brian Kidd, who scored a second goal. Ironically, Kidd had been told he was one of six players not included in the final World Cup squad of twenty-two. It was during a stop-over back in Bogota on the flight to Mexico that Bobby was arrested on the trumped-up jewel-theft charge following an allegation that he had stolen a bracelet from the hotel shop.

BOBBY: ❝This was the match in which Alf experimented with substitutions, preparing himself for any changes that might be required during the World Cup. The substitute rule was something new to Alf because it didn't exist when he was playing or as a club manager with Ipswich. I was delighted with my own personal game as I prepared to return to Mexico for the World Cup. Then came the crazy arrest ...❞

Alf Ramsey said on arriving in Mexico without Bobby Moore in his squad, "I will not be happy until my captain is back with us."

Chapter 13: The Beautiful Game

NEVER has there been a World Cup to equal the quality, the excitement and the drama of the 1970 finals in Mexico. Those of us lucky to be there considered ourselves privileged to be witnesses of football that touched perfection, and in particular to watch a Brazilian team that brought us a game from the Gods. Yes, the Beautiful Game. By the end of the incredible soccer jamboree, the names of their Famous Five forwards – Jairzinho, Gerson, Tostao, Pele and Rivelino – were rolling off our tongues like old friends. And our hero Bobby Moore, after all that he had been through with the jewel-theft sting, managed to walk tall out of the tournament with his reputation as being the Great Defender strengthened and now set in stone for all time.

BOBBY: ‘If I was asked to select the greatest England team with which I played I would not go for the 1966 World Cup winners but for the side I was proud to lead in the 1970 finals. There is no doubt in my mind that this team had more strength in depth than when we won the World Cup, and if we'd had a little luck I'm convinced we could have at least got to the final in our defence of the title. We got closest to mastering that great Brazilian team, and we had much the better of West Germany until we messed it up in the closing stages.’

CAP 81
Romania, World Cup, Guadalajara, 2.6.70. England won 1-0
Banks Newton (Wright) Cooper Mullery Labone   Moore*
Lee (Osgood) Ball   Charlton R. Hurst[1] Peters

Highlights: England started their World Cup defence as they had finished it in 1966, with Geoff Hurst emerging as the goal-scoring hero. His goal in the seventieth minute – the ball going through the legs of the Romanian goalkeeper – was enough to give England a winning send-off. Captain Bobby Moore, back with the squad after his harrowing experience in Colombia, was the outstanding defender on the pitch. It was a satisfactory rather than spectacular start by England against opponents who concentrated solely on defence in a bid to squeeze a draw out of a hard-fought match.

The one worry for England was an injury to right-back Keith Newton, but his Everton clubmate Tommy Wright proved a sound substitute.

> *BOBBY*: ❛This was the first substitution that Alf had to make in a World Cup match. Tommy slipped in comfortably as partner to Terry Cooper, and we were always in control against a side that took no prisoners with their tackling. I was just glad to be back playing after my ordeal in Bogota. As far as I was concerned, that was now history.❜

CAP 82
Brazil, World Cup, Guadalajara, 7.6.70. England lost 1-0
Banks Wright Cooper Mullery Labone Moore*
Lee (Astle) Ball Charlton R. (Bell) Hurst Peters

Highlights: An astonishing save by Gordon Banks from a header by Pele inspired England and found its way into the land of footballing legend. The game was staged in the heat of the mid-day sun on a scorching Sunday that was ideally suited for a siesta rather than soccer. Only mad dogs and footballers would have gone out in such sweltering 98-degree conditions, and at a thin-air altitude that made walking let alone running a challenge. The match was just ten minutes old and goalless when the master of all strikers – Pele – came face to face with a genius among goalkeepers – Gordon Banks – in a High Noon duel. Carlos Alberto, Brazilian right-back and captain, pushed a carefully calculated pass down the right wing into the path of the skilled Jairzinho, who suddenly and dramatically accelerated past Terry Cooper to the bye-line. He then stabbed a centre into the goalmouth that seemed to hang invitingly for Pele, who had instinctively read the situation as only he could. He had got himself perfectly positioned beyond his marker Alan Mullery to meet the ball. The master climbed above the ball and headed it with ferocious power down – and so he thought – into the net. Mullery later reported that Pele shouted 'Goal!' as the ball flew off his head. So did most spectators in the stadium, including the commentators sending their descriptive phrases around the world to millions of television viewers and radio listeners. Banks looked rooted on the wrong side of goal but suddenly, with the blurring speed of a panther, sprinted and then dived to his right and somehow managed to get an outstretched hand under the ball to flick it up and away over the bar. Pele stopped dead in mid-celebration to mourn what had somehow become a missed chance. This moment of astounding gymnastics from Banks inspired England to give the eventual world champions their hardest match of the tournament, but after a magnificent battle they finally succumbed to a superbly drilled shot by Jairzinho on the hour. He cut in from the right to score after an arrowing Tostao pass and a deft,

Pele and Bobby were team-mates for Team USA against England

perfectly delivered ball from Pele had ripped open the middle of the England defence. There was a memorable moment almost in the Pele/Banks class when Bobby Moore made one of the greatest tackles ever seen on the World Cup stage to stop another incisive run by Jaizinho. The England skipper timed his challenge to such perfection that many years later coaches were still showing film of the action as an example of how to tackle. Bobby then started a counter attack from which Jeff Astle had a gilt-edged chance to equalise within moments of coming on as a substitute but – yes, even in those heatwave conditions – he was caught cold and shot tamely wide. A lasting memory of the match for all those lucky enough to have witnessed the classic confrontation is of Bobby Moore and Pele cuddling each other before swapping shirts, two masters of the game recognising each other's genius. Evidence that the England players had given their all is that several of them lost up to ten pounds in weight after running round in the mid-day sun so that the World Cup organizers could satisfy the deadline demands of the great god of world-wide television. The millions tuned into the match will always recall it for having seen one of the saves and one of the tackles of the century.

BOBBY: ❝I was getting ready to pick the ball out of the net when Gordon appeared out of nowhere. He swooped across the goal like Superman and must have set some sort of world speed record getting from his near post to the far post. Was it a bird? Was it a plane? No, it was Banksie! What a pity we lost the game, because Gordon didn't deserve to be on the losing side after making a save like that. It was out of this world! It was one of the greatest games in which I ever played, and I was proud to be part of it even though we lost.❞

EYEWITNESS PELE

I just couldn't believe it when Gordon stopped my header. It was the biggest surprise I ever had on a football pitch. I have seen it many times on television and at the cinema and I am always astonished that he managed to save it. Not only was it incredible that he got to the ball but even more incredible that he managed to push it up and over the bar. I have met Gordon many times since and I always tell him that I scored more than 1000 goals but the only one people want to talk about is the one that he saved!

CAP 83

Czechoslovakia, World Cup, Guadalajara, 11.6.70. England won 1-0

Banks Newton Cooper Mullery Charlton J. Moore*
Bell Charlton R. (Ball) Astle (Osgood) Clarke[1p] Peters

Highlights: Allan Clarke volunteered for penalty duty in his first England international appearance, and showed an ice-cool temperament as he slotted home a disputed forty-eighth minute spot-kick that clinched a place in the World Cup quarter-finals. The only time the Czechs looked like scoring was when a speculative shot from twenty-five yards by right-back Dobias swerved in the thin air. Banks, at full stretch, managed to tip it on to the bar and as he turned the ball rebounded into his arms. It was a stuttering performance by England, but they had managed to reach the quarter-finals where waiting for them were, of all teams, West Germany.

BOBBY: ❛It was not often that you saw us laughing in the World Cup because it was a serious business. But when Gordon caught the ball as it bounced into his arms off the bar I said, "Great catch, Gordon. Now can you go to first slip."❜

CAP 84

West Germany, World Cup, Leon, 14.6.70. England lost 3-2 (aet)

Bonetti Newton Cooper Mullery[1] Labone Moore*
Lee Ball Charlton R. (Bell) Hurst Peters[1] (Hunter)

Highlights: There was a devastating blow to England when at the last minute goalkeeper Gordon Banks had to withdraw because of a stomach upset. Montezumah's revenge had never been harsher, robbing England of the best goalkeeper in the world. Peter Bonetti, who had not played a full competitive match since the end of the previous club season, was called in as emergency deputy. England were in command for sixty nine minutes thanks to goals from Alan Mullery and Martin Peters in stifling conditions. Franz Beckenbauer pulled the Germans back into the game with a shot that Bonetti would have saved nine times out of ten. Sir Alf Ramsey immediately sent on Colin Bell as substitute for Bobby Charlton, who was being saved for a semi-final that never came England's way. German substitute Jurgen Grabowski was running rings round exhausted left-back Terry Cooper, and Ramsey decided on a second substitution, sending on Norman Hunter for Peters in a bid to stiffen the defence. With Charlton and Peters off, it meant England had lost their two most composed players and suddenly they were looking disjointed. A freak header by Uwe Seeler sent the ball on an arc over the wrong-footed Bonetti to send the game into extra-time just as in the 1966

World Cup final, but this time it was the Germans who came out on top. Geoff Hurst had a goal disallowed, and then Gerd Muller rammed in the winner after Grabowski had beaten Cooper and crossed for Loehr to head the ball down into 'Der Bomber's' path. England's reign as world champions was over, as was the great international career of Bobby Charlton after a record 106 caps. Several of the England players were in tears, and Sir Alf was shell shocked. He did not believe it possible that any team could come back from two goals down against the England defence. How different it might have been had Gordon Banks been fit, and how different it might have been had Sir Alf not made a mess of his substitutions.

BOBBY: ❛It was a heartbreaking way to lose. Alf got it all wrong with the substitutions. Trying to save Bobby Charlton for the semi-final gave the Germans a huge lift, because seeing him go off was a bonus. Suddenly Beckenbauer felt a free man and started to dominate. Then sending Norman on for Martin unbalanced us. But it was losing Gordon before a ball was kicked that really did for us. With the greatest respect to Peter Bonetti, I know Gordon would not have let in two of those goals. When we returned to the hotel he was sitting up in bed watching a recording of the match and we were 2-0 up. He thought we were pulling his leg when we told him we had lost.❜

**EYEWITNESS
FRANZ
BECKENBAUER**

We could not believe it when England took off Bobby Charlton. He was a truly world class player, and we knew it improved our chances of saving the game when he went to the bench. We were so exhausted by the match that three days later we ran out of energy and lost 4-3 in extra-time to Italy in the semi-final. I talked about the tournament many times afterwards to my good friends, the two Bobbys, both of them wonderful sportsmen as well as great, great footballers. We all agreed Brazil were the team that year which deserved to take the world Cup. They were exceptional.

It was a tournament in which football was the winner, and Brazil showed why it was called the Beautiful Game. World Cup 1970. Never to be forgotten.

BACK in the world of club football, Bobby's strained relationship with West Ham manager Ron Greenwood came close to breaking point after the 1970-71 Blackpool Affair that we covered in the Mooro and Greavsie chapter. Bobby was fined a week's wages – £200 – and suspended for two weeks. What hurt him even more was that Alf Ramsey dropped him from the England team that played Malta in a European championship qualifying match.

BOBBY: ❛We were wrong to go to Brian London's nightclub, but we honestly believed the next day's match was going to be called off because of the heavy snow. Yes it was unprofessional, but they were unusual circumstances and we were in a relaxed New Year's Day mood. Our biggest 'crime' was losing the match. Ron could easily have kept it as an internal disciplinary matter, but chose to tell the world. To be honest, I lost a lot of respect for him over that decision. And I felt Alf could have shown me more loyalty. But I blame myself. I should not have gone to the nightclub.❜

CAP 85
East Germany, Wembley, 25.11.70. England won 3-1
Shilton   Hughes   Cooper   Mullery   Sadler   Moore*
Lee[1]   Ball   Hurst   Clarke[1]   Peters[1]

Highlights: Peter Shilton won the first of his record 125 caps against an inventive East German team that had scored sixteen goals winning their previous four matches. They could make little impression against an experimental England defence as Sir Alf started rebuilding with the 1972 European championships in mind. Manchester United's utility player David Sadler patrolled alongside the maestro Bobby Moore in the middle of the defence, and Emlyn Hughes partnered Terry Cooper at full back. Sir Alf reverted to his favourite 4-3-3 formation, with Allan Clarke joining Francis Lee and Geoff Hurst at the front. Lee and Martin Peters gave England a 2-0 lead inside the first twenty minutes, and the cool, calculating Clarke clinched an impressive victory midway through the second-half after the East Germans had pulled a goal back with a dipping twenty-five yard drive by Vogel that caught Shilton off his line.

It was five weeks later that there was, for want of a better word, a hiccup in Bobby's club and country career when he went for the New Year's Day drink in Blackpool. Among his companions was a player I watched as a free-scoring West Ham schoolboy and in 1965 I reported his five First Division goals in 20 minutes against West Bromwich Albion ... affectionately known as Stag ... Brian Dear. He hero worshipped Bobby ...

**EYEWITNESS
BRIAN
DEAR**

That Blackpool business was blown out of all proportion, and I felt West Ham treated their greatest player appallingly. Most people know the legendary stories of Bobby Moore the footballer, but I knew Bobby Moore the man, because he was my good pal. Being part of the famous West Ham United Academy was an amazing experience in itself. Even though there were only two years between Bobby and me it was obvious to all of us that Bobby was in a different league. Having achieved all that he did in the game he had every reason to look down on us but he never did; in fact it was quite the opposite. He had time for everyone and he had a knack of making you feel comfortable in whatever circumstance or company we were in. I remember standing in the tunnel at Wembley before the Cup Winners Cup Final in 1965 and I was extremely nervous. Bobby sensed my anxiety and just said to me to walk behind him as he led the team out ... "that way you will at least be in all of the photos!" That comment made me smile and in an instant calmed my nerves. I was close friends with Bobby until he left us and I have so many memories of him on the training ground and on the pitch, but for me the greatest memories are of our friendship. Bowel cancer is a terrible disease and I am proud that his name is doing so much to help so many even after his death. He was truly a class act and still is; I miss him every day. They definitely don't make them like him anymore. Extraordinary footballer, great human being.

Bobby was not only suspended by West Ham over the Blackpool Affair, but Alf Ramsey left him out of the England squad for the European championship match in Malta, which to neutrals seemed a bit over the top for a player who had given his all for his club and country.

Malta, Valletta, 3.2.71. England won 1-0

Banks   Reaney   Hughes   Mullery*   McFarland   Hunter
Ball   Chivers   Royle   Harvey   Peters[1]

Highlights: Alan Mullery was skipper in place of Bobby Moore, who had been suspended by his West Ham club following the 'Blackpool Affair.' Martin Chivers, Roy McFarland and Everton team-mates Joe Royle and Colin Harvey made their debuts in a European championship qualifying match played on an iron-hard pitch that Gordon Banks described as 'the worst I have ever seen.' It had a sand surface that had been rolled flat by a steam-roller. Martin Peters scored the only goal after half a dozen chances had been missed.

CAP 86

Greece, Wembley, 21.4.71. England won 3-0

Banks   Storey   Hughes   Mullery   McFarland   Moore*
Lee[1]   Ball (Coates)   Chivers[1]   Hurst[1]   Peters

Highlights: Greece arrived for this European championship qualifying match without any of the their star players from Panathinaikos, who were being saved for a European Cup semi-final. A superbly struck goal by Martin Chivers was all that separated the teams at half-time, and it took late headed goals by Geoff Hurst and Francis Lee to clinch victory and silence the jeers of a frustrated crowd. Peter Storey got his first England call up as reward for his consistent performances for an Arsenal team on the way to a League and FA Cup double.

BOBBY: 'This was such a frustrating game. The Greeks came only to defend and hid their goal behind a human wall. I could understand the supporters getting annoyed because they had paid good money to see two teams play a game of football. But only we were interested in trying to win. Gordon Banks did not have a single shot to save, and the only time he got to touch the ball was when we passed it back to him.'

CAPS 87

Malta, Wembley, 12.5.71. England won 5-0

Banks   Lawler[1]   Cooper   Moore*   McFarland   Hughes
Lee[1]   Coates   Chivers[2]   Clarke[1]   Peters (Ball)

Highlights: Allan Clarke scored one penalty and missed another and Martin Chivers netted twice and might have had five goals. Francis Lee was on the mark, and Chris Lawler decorated his debut with a spectacular long-range goal from thirty yards. But it was not enough to please the 36,500 spectators who jeered and slow-handclapped England's performance in this return European championship match.

> BOBBY: ❛Malta were even less ambitious than the Greeks had been and never came out of their half. Gordon was once again redundant and called me over and asked me if I could smell bacon! This got into the papers, and somebody wrote to Gordon to tell him he'd been eating bacon sandwiches behind his goal.❜

CAP 88
Northern Ireland, Windsor Park, 15.5.71. England won 1-0
Banks Madeley Cooper Storey McFarland Moore*
Lee Ball Chivers Clarke[1] Peters

Highlights: George Best had an opportunist goal disallowed after flicking the ball away from Gordon Banks as the England goalkeeper threw it up in preparation for a kicked clearance. Many people considered it a magical piece of skill and impudence by Best, but Scottish referee MacKenzie decided he had been guilty of dangerously high kicking and, much to the annoyance of Best and the crowd, he awarded England a free-kick. Allan Clarke's winning goal ten minutes from the end brought off-side claims from the Irish defenders who also insisted that Francis Lee had handled the ball before passing to Clarke. It was not Ireland's lucky day. Paul Madeley, Leeds United's versatile defender, came in at right back as Sir Alf continued to search for the perfect blend and balance at full back.

> BOBBY: ❛That genius George Best deserved a goal for being so inventive, but Gordon understandably said the referee was right to disallow the goal because it would have encouraged players to kick high against goalkeepers. I had never seen George so angry. That suited us, because while he was so busy arguing it meant he wasn't concentrating on playing.❜

Wales, Wembley, 19.5.71. Drew 0-0
Shilton Lawler Cooper Smith Lloyd Hughes
Lee Coates Hurst Brown (Clarke) Peters*

Highlights: Sir Alf Ramsey's experimental side played like passing strangers in the face of a fierce challenge from Wales. England included new caps Larry Lloyd, Tommy Smith and Tony Brown, whose only appearance for England lasted just seventy-four

George Best, the Irish genius who was Bobby's footballing and drinking pal

minutes before he was replaced by substitute Allan Clarke. Francis Lee had a goal ruled off side in the 43rd minute. Martin Peters captained England for the first time in place of rested Bobby Moore, whose poise and authority was greatly missed in England's back line.

CAP 89
Scotland, Wembley, 22.5.71. England won 3-1
Banks   Lawler   Cooper   Storey   McFarland   Moore*
Lee (Clarke)   Ball   Chivers² Hurst   Peters¹

Highlights: Martin Peters headed England into the lead before Alan Ball gifted Scotland an equaliser with a suicidal back pass into the path of Hugh Curran. Ball made amends with a storming performance in midfield, and two Martin Chivers goals gave England victory and the home international championship.

> *BOBBY*: ❛The hordes of Scottish fans in the Wembley crowd turned their anger on manager Bobby Brown and kept up a non-stop chant of 'If you hate Bobby Brown, clap your hands.' Alf showed his human side by putting a comforting arm around Brown's shoulders as they walked to the dressing-rooms at the end. Alf was a much warmer and caring person than his public image suggested. What a pity he lacked communication skills.❜

CAP 90
Switzerland, Basle, 13.10.71. England won 3-2 (own goal¹)
Banks   Lawler   Cooper   Mullery   McFarland   Moore*
Lee   Madeley   Chivers¹ Hurst¹ (Radford)   Peters

Highlights: Two rare mistakes by Gordon Banks let Switzerland in for equalisers after England had twice taken the lead through goals by Geoff Hurst and Martin Chivers in the first-half of this European championship qualifier. It was just looking as if the Swiss would escape with a draw when a Chivers cross was deflected into the net by defender Weibel for a seventy-ninth minute winner. The victory put England top of their qualifying group.

> *BOBBY*: ❛One of the Swiss goals was as much down to me as to Gordon. For one of the few times in all the matches we had played together I got in his way as he came for a cross and it led to a simple goal for the Swiss. Alf tore into us at the end over our clumsy play, but as usual he did it in private. He never ripped into his players in public, another reason we respected him.❜

CAPS 91
Switzerland, Wembley, 10.11.71. Drew 1-1
Shilton Madeley Cooper Storey Lloyd Moore*
Summerbee[1] (Chivers) Ball Hurst Lee (Marsh) Hughes

Highlights: Mike Summerbee gave England the lead in the ninth minute, but then they struggled to contain a lively Swiss team that deserved their equaliser, hammered in from twenty-five yards by Odermatt in the twenty-sixth minute. It was a swinging shot that spun into the net off Shilton's hands. England's passing was often careless, and Sir Alf Ramsey responded to the crowd chants of 'Rod-ney, Rod-ney' by sending on Queen's Park Rangers cult hero Rodney Marsh for his England debut as substitute for Summerbee, the player he would soon join as a clubmate at Manchester City.

BOBBY: ❝Only a defeat by four or more goals in our final qualifying match in Greece could stop us reaching the quarter-finals of the European championship. Alf warned us not to become complacent, and made it clear to the press that he would be selecting his strongest possible side for the game in Athens. We all wondered whether that would mean a recall for Gordon Banks.❞

CAP 92
Greece, Athens, 1.12.71. England won 2-0
Banks Madeley Hughes Bell McFarland Moore*
Lee Ball Chivers[1] Hurst[1] Peters

Highlights: A cannonball shot from Geoff Hurst midway through the first-half put England in charge of a match dominated by the attacking midfield trio of Alan Ball, Colin Bell and Martin Peters. Martin Chivers wrapped up the victory with a last-minute goal to clinch England's place in the quarter-finals of the European championship. Francis Lee twice hit the post, and the final scoreline flattered a Greek team which was under the management of 1958 Northern Ireland World Cup hero Billy Bingham, who had been a huge favourite in England when playing for Everton.

BOBBY: ❝That always cheerful man Billy Bingham came into our dressing-room and shook every player's hand while congratulating us. He told Alf that he was convinced England were good enough to go on and win the European championship. We shared his confidence, even though waiting for us in the quarter-finals were my old mate Franz Beckenbauer's West German side, and a re-match at Wembley.❞

We take a breather from Bobby's England assignments to dip into one of his most demanding challenges with West Ham. Come with me back to the astonishing 1971-72 League Cup semi-final serial between Stoke City and the Hammers that had more twists and turns and drama than an Alfred Hitchcock thriller. This was *Psycho* meets *Frenzy*, with *The 39 Steps* of Wembley waiting for the winners.

The scheduled two-leg semi-final stretched to four matches, and seven hours of football fought with a pace and a passion that you rarely see in today's more sanitized and sane – and dare I say, soulless – game.

Let's take it a match at a time.

The first leg was played at Stoke's Victoria Ground on December 8 1971, and a 36,407 crowd saw the Hammers hurry and hustle Stoke to a 2-1 defeat. A 14th minute Peter Dobing goal for Stoke was cancelled out – and make a note of this – by a Geoff Hurst penalty, with Clyde Best scoring a winning goal that had Hammers fans rehearsing choruses of Bubbles for their anticipated appearance at Wembley.

Stoke manager Tony Waddington, the master motivator who specialised in pumping life back into footballers considered past their sell-by date, said: "We've given ourselves a mountain to climb, but we have experienced players in our side who have a head for heights. This is just half-time. I am still confident that we can take that big step to Wembley."

The teams:
STOKE: Banks, Marsh, Pejic, Bernard, Bloor, Jump, Conroy, Greenhoff, Ritchie, Dobing, Eastham.

WEST HAM: Ferguson, McDowell, Lampard, Bonds, Taylor, Moore, Redknapp, Best, Hurst, Brooking, Robson.

The second leg at Upton Park seven days later attracted a heaving crowd of 38,771, and a John Ritchie goal in the 72nd minute took the game into extra-time. A third match was beckoning when two minutes from the final whistle Gordon Banks had a rare rush of blood to the head and pulled down 24-year-old West Ham winger Harry Redknapp in the penalty area.

It was like a repeat of a high noon shoot out – okay, it was nearer 10pm under the Upton Park floodlights – as Geoff Hurst placed the ball on the penalty spot ready to take aim against his 1966 World Cup team-mate.

A few years later I ghosted Gordon's *Banks of England* autobiography. This is how he described the moment:

'In the first leg Geoff had beaten me all ends up after taking a Freddie Trueman style run-up before powering the ball into the net to my right and at about shoulder height. This penalty was still in my mind as I faced Geoff again from the spot at Upton Park. I was having to bring my emotions under control because I knew that I was to blame for the penalty, stupidly pulling down Harry Redknapp as he tried to run the ball past me. If you could have seen the looks on the faces of my Stoke team-mates you would have thought they could have willingly put me up against a wall in front of a firing squad. A minute later they were gleefully trying to carry me around the pitch as if I was the League Cup after I had somehow managed to save Geoff's penalty.

I noticed that he was taking exactly the same length and angled run to the ball as in the first match at Stoke, so I decided I would dive to my right in the hope and belief that the ball would be driven to the same spot as before. My calculations could not have been better. I got to the ball with my outstretched right hand and it was moving with such force that it bounced up against the bar and high away into the crowd for a corner.

To be honest, I rate the save nearly up there with the one against Pelé in the World Cup. Geoff was astonished, and said to me later that he had never hit a ball harder from the penalty spot and he thought that if I got a touch it would knock me back into the net. I could feel the sting of the ball on my hand for hours afterwards.

We felt we had come back from the dead, and now we were determined to get through to the final. It was, we decided, our destiny.'

The teams:
WEST HAM: Ferguson, McDowell, Lampard, Bonds, Taylor, Moore, Redknapp, Best, Hurst, Brooking, Robson.
STOKE: Banks, Marsh, Pejic, Bernard, Bloor, Skeels, Conroy, Greenhoff, Ritchie, Dobing, Eastham (Mahoney).

The Hammers/Stoke roadshow, with the teams locked on a 2-2 aggregate score, moved on to Sheffield for the third stage of the marathon, followed by 46,196 spectators for the match at Hillsborough on January 5 1972. Both teams walked a tightrope of tension and there were alarms and panic in each goalmouth during a goalless slog that went to extra-time. Playing time to date: 5 hours 30 minutes.

West Ham's Geordie striker Bryan 'Pop' Robson thought he had broken the deadlock, but was robbed by that man Banks, who stretched across goal to make what we mere mortals would consider a spectacular save but to Gordon was just bread and butter.

Managers Tony Waddington and Ron Greenwood tossed for a south or north venue for chapter four in the serial, and the Stoke manager won and plumped for Old Trafford as the stage for the next meeting on January 26 1972. Terrace prices were set at 35p to save the near-exhausted supporters from having to dig any deeper into their over-stretched pockets.

The teams:

STOKE: Banks, Marsh, Pejic, Bernard, Smith, Bloor, Conroy, Dobing, Ritchie, Greenhoff (Skeels), Eastham.

WEST HAM: Ferguson, McDowell, Lampard, Bonds, Taylor, Moore, Redknapp, Best, Hurst, Brooking, Robson.

The final act of the seven-hour drama in front of 49,247 fans produced five goals, a 3-2 victory for Stoke and a penalty save by, of all people, Bobby Moore. My press box colleague Peter Batt summed it up for his *Sun* readers much better than I could: "The most exciting game I have ever seen."

As torrential rain soaked the players and spectators, Scottish goalkeeper Bobby Ferguson was badly concussed in the 13th minute by a kick in the head from Terry Conroy as they battled for the ball on a mud-caked surface. The loose ball went into the net but the referee ruled it out and awarded a free-kick to West Ham, whose players were fuming over the Conroy challenge. Ferguson was treated for 13 minutes, tried to resume but was staggering around on the goal-line like an Embankment drunk before being led off on legs of jelly.

Minutes later emergency goalkeeper Moore – this in the days of just one substitute – was facing a penalty from Mike Bernard, and he dived to parry the ball. The West Ham and England skipper did not deserve to have Bernard following up to to bundle in the rebound to give Stoke a 1-0 lead, 3-2 on aggregate.

The still groggy Ferguson – who later said he had no recall of the match – returned between the posts as West Ham fought back in a game that everybody else would recall as an epic. The magnificent Billy Bonds had a 40th minute equaliser deflected past Banks, and then Trevor Brooking spectacularly volleyed West Ham ahead from a Bonds cross at the start of the injury time added for Ferguson's treatment.

Dobing made it 2-2 in the last minute of a frantic first-half that eventually ran 15 minutes overtime. Referee Pat Partridge was looking like a drowned rat as he at last blew the whistle.

It was Conroy, jeered and booed by the West Ham fans every time he touched the ball, who scored what was to prove the winning goal four minutes into the second-half, A fit Ferguson would have saved his shot, but he dived through his fog far too late as the ball skidded just inside the post for what was a tame decider to a momentous match fought in Somme-like conditions.

Harry Redknapp, skipping across the pitch like a twelve-year-old mudlark, twice hit the Stoke woodwork and Geoff Hurst had two shots saved by his Nemesis Gordon Banks as the Hammers battled gloriously to try to prolong the action.

The West Ham fans left Old Trafford with tears as well as rain streaming down their faces at the end of one of the great football serials that had been watched by 171,341 spectators. For Stoke – Dad's Army – the Wembley dream was still alive.

Gordon Banks, always alert at his post for Stoke and England

The teams:

STOKE: Banks, Marsh, Pejic, Bernard, Smith, Bloor, Conroy, Greenhoff, Ritchie, Dobing, Eastham.

WEST HAM: Ferguson, McDowell, Lampard, Bonds, Taylor, Moore, Redknapp (Eustace), Best, Hurst, Brooking, Robson.

On March 4 1972, Stoke beat Chelsea 2-1 in the final, with Matchstick Man George Eastham scoring a fairytale winner in his last season in the Football League before emigrating to South Africa. It was Stoke skipper Peter Dobing who led the Potteries players up those 39 Wembley steps to collect the club's first trophy in their 108-year history. Even Hitchcock could not have conjured this climax.

Gordon Banks was rewarded for his stupendous goalkeeping by being elected Footballer of the Year. In October the following season he tragically lost the sight of an eye in a car crash, and his glittering career was all but over apart from a season in the North American Soccer League when, amazingly, he was voted the Most Valuable Player.

For anybody who did not see him play, let me just say if he was at his peak in the modern game he would be football's first £30-million goalkeeper.

All these years later I can reveal that Bobby Moore had tried to persuade Ron Greenwood to sign Banks for the Hammers when, in 1967, Leicester City decided to let him go because they had the young and hungry Peter Shilton waiting in the wings.

Greenwood was equally keen, but because he was a man of principle he kept his word with Kilmarnock and went ahead with his world record £65,000 deal for Scottish international goalkeeper Bobby Ferguson. Now *that* Fergie would recall.

Banks moved to Stoke City for £52,000, and five years later produced the astonishing penalty save that broke West Ham hearts and left Geoff Hurst shaking his head in disbelief.

BOBBY: ❝I called for volunteers to go into goal when Fergie was so badly concussed he did not know what day it was. Nobody put their hand up so I decided to do the job myself. I'd played once in goal in a reserve game and also briefly in a first-team match at Chelsea. I'd never let a goal in so I had a 100 per cent record as I faced Mike Bernard's penalty. He didn't connect properly and the ball came towards me at waist height. It hit my palms and bounced back into Bernard's path and he scrambled it home, with me diving around like a fish out of water. While I was choked for us, I was delighted for little George Eastham, who went on to at last get the Wembley final that he deserved. People forget the part he played in getting our wages improved by going on strike at Newcastle. How could I begrudge him a League Cup trophy?❞

CAP 93
West Germany, Wembley, 29.4.72. England lost 3-1
Banks Madeley Hughes Bell Moore* Hunter
Lee[1] Ball Chivers Hurst (Marsh) Peters

Highlights: Derby manager Brian Clough pulled slightly injured Roy McFarland out of the England squad at the last minute, and Sir Alf Ramsey's gamble of playing Bobby Moore at centre-half in his place was a tactical disaster in this European championship quarter-final. Moore and Norman Hunter were always struggling at the heart of the defence against the dynamic Gerd Muller, who fed off a procession of passes from the gifted schemer Gunter Netzer. Francis Lee equalised a twenty-sixth minute goal by Uli Hoeness, and outplayed England clung on until six minutes from the end when Netzer scored from the penalty spot. Moments later Muller made it 3-1 with a devastating shot on the turn. It left England with a mountain to climb in the second leg in Germany.

> *BOBBY*: ❛I was as surprised as everybody else when Alf decided to play Norman and me together in the middle of the defence. Neither of us was a centre-half and neither of us was ever commanding in the air. We thought too much alike about our positioning and kept going for the same ball. All in all it was one of the most disappointing and depressing internationals in which I ever played. We were murdered by the passing of Gunter Netzer and the power of Gerd Muller.❜

CAP 94
West Germany, Berlin, 13.5.72. Drew 0-0
Banks Madeley Hughes Storey McFarland Moore*
Ball Bell Chivers Marsh (Summerbee) Hunter (Peters)

Highlights: Franz Beckenbauer, playing a sweeper role, was outstanding as the German defence shut out England's attack in a match contested in a non-stop downpour. The Germans, content to protect their two-goal lead from the first leg, came closest to breaking the deadlock when a 40-yard free-kick from Netzer smacked against the bar. England, with Norman Hunter and Peter Storey literally making their presence felt, conceded twenty-seven free-kicks and were described by German manager Helmut Schoen as 'brutal'. For Sir Alf Ramsey the 1974 World Cup finals in Germany now became all-important. His enemies at the FA were gathering like vultures. Only four of the 'Old Guard' were left in his squad – Banks, Moore, Ball and Peters.

BOBBY: ❛We went to Berlin in a negative state of mind and the awful weather suited our mood. It was the most physical team Alf had ever picked, and Netzer said later that we had all taken turns to autograph his legs. It was not pretty, and in truth the Germans deserved to go through. It was all down to our poor performance at Wembley.❜

CAP 95
Wales, Ninian Park, 20.5.72. England won 3-0
Banks Madeley Hughes[1] Storey McFarland Moore*
Summerbee Bell[1] Macdonald Marsh[1] Hunter

Highlights: England cruised to a comfortable victory in a bruising Home Championship match in which Peter Storey and Terry Yorath, two of the hardest men in the League, had a personal feud, with Norman Hunter often joining in on Storey's side against his Leeds clubmate. Leading 1-0 from a first-half goal by Emlyn Hughes, England clinched victory with two goals in a minute midway through the second-half. Rodney Marsh scored with a first-time volley from eighteen yards, and then Mike Summerbee laid on the third goal for his Manchester City team-mate Colin Bell. Malcolm Macdonald made a bright debut in the number nine England shirt.

BOBBY: ❛Storey and Yorath took a history of incidents at club level into this match, and it was ugly to watch as they went for each other throughout the match. The referee kept turning a blind eye, and both were lucky not to get a red card. As we came off at the end we had to pull them apart in the players' tunnel. Neither would give an inch. I think it fair to say they did not like each other.❜

Northern Ireland, Wembley, 23.5.72. England lost 1-0
Shilton Todd Hughes Storey Lloyd Hunter
Summerbee Bell* Macdonald (Chivers) Marsh Currie (Peters)

Highlights: This was England's first defeat by Northern Ireland since 1957. Terry Neill, the Irish player-manager winning his fiftieth cap, scored the only goal of the match from close range following a Danny Hegan corner in the thirty-third minute. Colin Bell skippered England in the absence of injured Bobby Moore, and Tony Currie and Colin Todd won their first caps. It was the first match since the 1966 World Cup that England kicked off without one of the heroes of '66 in the starting line-up, with Martin Peters coming on as a substitute to show the era was not quite over.

CAP 96

Scotland, Hampden Park, 27.5.72. England won 1-0

Banks Madeley Hughes Storey McFarland Moore*

Ball[1] Bell Chivers Marsh (Macdonald) Hunter

Highlights: The referee called captains Bobby Moore and Billy McNeill together and ordered them to tell their warring players to calm things down after 46 free-kicks in the first 30 minutes. An Alan Ball goal in the 28th minute gave England victory in this daggers-drawn centenary match between the two countries. Peter Storey and Norman Hunter were at the heart of the trouble with their fierce tackling, and this brought out the competitive spirit in the likes of Billy Bremner, Bobby Moncur and Denis Law. Several players seemed more intent on kicking each other rather than the ball.

BOBBY: ❛The referee warned Billy and me that if we didn't tell our team-mates to cut out the violence he'd take us all off. It was completely out of control in the first-half. Billy told the ref that England had started it, and there were several Scots who were in the mood to finish it! It's a wonder we finished with eleven a side. Definitely the roughest home international in which I played.❜

CAP 97

Yugoslavia, Wembley, 11.10.72. Drew 1-1

Shilton Mills Lampard Storey Blockley Moore*

Ball Channon Royle[1] Bell Marsh

Highlights: Mick Mills, Frank Lampard (senior, of course), Jeff Blockley and Mike Channon made their international debuts as Sir Alf Ramsey juggled his squad because of club calls and injuries. The quartet of newcomers looked set for a winning start when Joe Royle scored his first goal for England in the fortieth minute, but Yugoslav centre-forward Franjo Vladic snatched an equaliser five minutes after half-time and Peter Shilton had to be at his best as skilful winger Dragan Djazic started to pull the uncertain England defence apart.

BOBBY: ❛It was tough luck on Mick Mills that he had to make his international debut against Djazic, one of the greatest players ever produced by Yugoslavia. He was a magnificent player, and gave poor Mick a real chasing. We knew we were lucky to get away with a draw.❜

Sir Alf and Bobby now got themselves geared for their last great challenge together:

Chapter 15: Polished Off By A Clown

SIR ALF and Bobby teamed up for one more campaign, this time for the 1974 World Cup finals that were scheduled for West Germany. The fact that it turned into a shambles and climaxed with a night of torment and torture at Wembley is one of the saddest chapters in England's international football history.

On paper, it looked as if England had every chance to get through to the World Cup finals. They were in a three-country qualifying group with Poland and Wales, and – before a ball was kicked – were red-hot favourites to go through. The opening match against Wales was a personal milestone for Sir Alf Ramsey, his 100th match in charge of England since taking over from Walter Winterbottom in 1963.

BOBBY: ❛We were determined not to take anything for granted, but we were quietly confident that we could see off Poland and Wales. Only Ballie, Martin Peters and I were left from the 1966 team, and we had loads of skill and class in our squad. I was very proud to be their captain and we wanted to mark Alf's centenary with a victory.❜

CAP 98
Wales, Ninian Park, 15.11.72. England won 1-0
Clemence Storey Hughes Hunter McFarland Moore*
Keegan Chivers Marsh Bell[1] Ball

Highlights: Colin Bell, the Marathon Man of football, cashed in on clever approach work by Alan Ball to score the decisive winning goal in the first-half of this opening World Cup qualifying match. Liverpool team-mates Ray Clemence and Kevin Keegan made quietly satisfactory debuts in what was Sir Alf Ramsey's 100th match as manager. A feature of the game was the way Peter Storey snuffed out the challenge of Wales match winner Leighton James with a controlled, man-to-man containing role. Keegan, conspicuous with his bubble-permed hair, had a golden opportunity to mark his debut with a last-minute goal, but Leeds goalkeeper Gary Sprake whipped the ball off his toes as he attempted to dribble the ball into the net. It was a memorable night for both Keegan and Clemence, who had each started their careers in the football outpost of Scunthorpe United.

BOBBY: ‘Alf, as usual, wanted no fuss made about his 100th international in charge of England. He said it had been marked in the best way possible, a victory. Our World Cup campaign was off to a winning start against one of the finest Welsh teams for years. We knew the return match would not be a walkover.’

CAP 99
Wales, Wembley, 24.1.73. Drew 1-1
Clemence Storey Hughes Hunter[1] McFarland Moore*
Keegan Bell Chivers Marsh Ball

Highlights: A long-range shot from Norman Hunter in the forty-second minute beat his Leeds team-mate Gary Sprake in the Welsh goal to salvage a World Cup point. John Toshack had given Wales the lead in the twenty-third minute after clever approach play by Leighton James, and England's forwards floundered against a Welsh defence in which Sprake, Peter Rodrigues and Mike England were outstanding. It was a disastrous point for England to drop on the way to the World Cup finals, and there was a much tougher obstacle ahead in the shape of Poland.

BOBBY: ‘We got crucified by the media for this display, and they were heaping criticism on Alf for being too negative with his tactics. But you could not blame Alf for the fact that we were unable to break down a magnificent Wales defence. They played out of their skin and we were fortunate to escape with a draw. Now we had it all to do against Poland.’

CAP 100
Scotland, Hampden Park, 14.2.73. England won 5-0 (own goal[1])
Shilton Storey Hughes Bell Madeley Moore*
Ball Channon[1] Chivers[1] Clarke[2] Peters

Highlights: England were three goals clear in 15 minutes, and skated to an easy victory on a snow-carpeted pitch. The match was played to celebrate the Centenary of the Scottish FA but England – with Bobby Moore making his 100th appearance – wrecked the party. It was a nightmare start to Willie Ormond's job as new Scottish manager, following in the shoes of Tommy Docherty. 'England hit the High Cs' was the tabloid headlines as Allan Clarke (2), former Southampton side-kicks Mike Channon and Martin Chivers shared the goals, and they were further helped by an own goal from Peter Lorimer on what was a totally embarrassing night for the Scots.

BOBBY: ❝I couldn't believe this was my hundredth game for England. It seemed just a blink of an eye ago that I was making my debut in Peru. The Scottish FA kindly made a special presentation and then we ran their players silly! We kept our feet much better on the ice rink of a pitch and destroyed them with our pace. It lifted our confidence after our poor performance against Wales. The press could hardly say we were negative.❞

CAP 101
Northern Ireland, Goodison Park, 12.5.73. England won 2-1
Shilton   Storey Nish Bell   McFarland Moore*
Ball   Channon   Chivers[2]   Richards Peters

Highlights: The game should have been played in Belfast but because of the political problems was switched to Goodison Park at the request of the Irish FA. A rare mistake by goalkeeper Pat Jennings let Martin Chivers in for his first goal in the ninth minute, and another mistake – this time by Terry Neill – set Chivers up for the winning goal nine minutes from the end. Dave Clements scored for Ireland from the penalty spot after a foul by Peter Storey in the twenty-second minute. Wolves striker John Richards won his only cap. England's disjointed display brought them jeers and slow handclaps from the Goodison crowd, the majority of whom seemed to be supporting the Irish.

BOBBY: ❝Although the game was played in England we felt we were in Ireland. The crowd could not have been more pro-Irish if we'd been playing in Windsor Park. We were untidy and lacked the rhythm and spark we'd produced against Scotland. The final score flattered us, but Martin Chivers deserved credit for taking the two chances that were presented to him.❞

CAP 102
Wales, Wembley, 15.5.73. England won 3-0
Shilton   Storey Hughes Bell McFarland   Moore*
Ball Channon[1] Chivers[1] Clarke   Peters[1]

Highlights: England scored three goals and had two others disallowed as they pulled the Welsh defence apart in this Home Championship match. Allan Clarke did not get his name on the scoresheet, but he was the outstanding player as he combined neatly with Mike Channon and Martin Chivers. It was England's first victory at Wembley for two years. Martin Peters saved the best until last, scoring with a swerving shot from twenty yards after neatly combining with Channon and Clarke to make an opening.

BOBBY: ❝If only we had produced this form against Wales in the World Cup qualifying match at Wembley. Sniffer Clarke was in exceptional form and pulled the Welsh defence to pieces with his pace and intelligent positioning. He didn't get the ball into the net but he was man of the match.❞

CAP 103
Scotland, Wembley, 19.5.73. England won 1-0
Shilton Storey Hughes Bell McFarland Moore*
Ball Channon Chivers Clarke Peters[1]

Highlights: Martin Peters headed in a beautifully flighted free-kick from Alan Ball in the fifty-fourth minute to give England victory in a hard-fought match that tested their stamina as much as their skill. The Scots might easily have won but for magnificent saves by Peter Shilton from Peter Lorimer and Kenny Dalglish. Scotland turned it into a physical battle, with Billy Bremner and big Jim Holton kicking anything that moved. England's win gave them their twenty-ninth Home Championship.

BOBBY: ❝This was the perfect result to put us in a confident mood for our summer tour that included a crucial World Cup qualifier against Poland. I always rated Gordon Banks the greatest goalkeeper I ever played with, but Shilts had the sort of game that made me wonder if perhaps I should change that assessment.❞

CAP 104
Czechoslovakia, Prague, 27.5.73. Drew 1-1
Shilton Madeley Storey Bell McFarland Moore*
Ball Channon Chivers Clarke[1] Peters

Highlights: Allan Clarke saved England from defeat with a last-minute equaliser after collecting the ball from his Leeds team-mate Paul Madeley. The Czechs led from the fifty-sixth minute when Novak steered the ball into the net off a post. England, unfamiliar in yellow shirts and royal-blue shorts and with Peter Storey playing out of position at left-back, lacked cohesion.

BOBBY: ❝Alf was furious because he felt we were lacking total commitment, with the thought of the Poland match on our minds. This friendly was arranged as a warm up for the World Cup qualifier, but all it did was put doubts in our minds.❞

Bobby with the man who would overtake his caps record, goalkeeper Peter Shilton

CAP 105
Poland, Chorzow, 6.6.73. England lost 2-0
Shilton   Madeley Hughes Storey   McFarland Moore*
Ball   Bell Chivers   Clarke Peters

Highlights: This was a disastrous defeat for England in a vital World Cup qualifying match. Poland went ahead in the ninth minute when a Lubanski shot found its way into the net off the foot of Bobby Moore and the arm of Peter Shilton. Early in the second-half Moore made an uncharacteristic hash of a tackle against Lubanski, who raced clear to make it 2-0. To compound England's misery Alan Ball was sent off following an angry clash twelve minutes from the final whistle. Once again, Sir Alf's poor understanding of the substitute system let down England. It screamed out for attacking players to be sent on when the Poles went two goals clear, but Ramsey stuck with his rigid 4-4-2 formation that meant the game became bogged down in midfield as Poland chose to close up shop and hang on to their lead.

BOBBY: ❛Not my finest hour. Lubanski, one of Europe's most dangerous forwards, intercepted the ball as I was trying to clear and sprinted away from me as I lost my balance. He drilled the ball past the oncoming Shilts with me as a spectator. It was probably my worst moment on a football pitch. It was the sort of clearance I had made a thousand times before, but just this once I made a mess of it. Alf came to my hotel room afterwards and we had a good drink and talked about what needed to be done to make sure we won the return match at Wembley.❜

CAP 106
USSR, Moscow, 10.6.73. England won 2-1 (own goal[1])
Shilton   Madeley Hughes Storey McFarland Moore*
Currie   Channon (Summerbee)   Chivers[1] Clarke (Macdonald)   Peters (Hunter)

Highlights: Just four days after the disappointment of defeat in Poland, England showed their character with a victory made harder by the stifling, humid conditions in the Lenin Stadium. Chivers powered England into the lead in the ninth minute, and ten minutes after half-time a clever dummy by Martin Peters so confused Russian defender Khurtislava that he turned the ball into his own net. The Russians pulled back a goal in the sixty-sixth minute from the penalty spot. Tony Currie was an impressive deputy for Alan Ball. Bobby Moore, equalling Bobby Charlton's record of 106 England caps, was back to his imperious best following his below-par performance in Poland.

BOBBY: ❛I don't know what some of the old Blazers at the FA expected from me in this match. The night before the game in Moscow I'd had my usual trouble sleeping and the hotel room was so stifling that I decided to go for a walk in a nearby park. It was the middle of the night. I sat on a park bench and nodded off to sleep. Two of our senior selection committee went for a breakfast-time stroll in the park and saw what they thought to be a tramp asleep on the bench. As I sat up they were shocked to find it was the England football captain. But I was wide awake for a game in which we played with some style.❜

CAP 107
Italy, Turin, 14.6.73. England lost 2-0
Shilton   Madeley   Hughes   Storey   McFarland   Moore*
Currie   Channon   Chivers   Clarke   Peters

Highlights: Bobby Moore set a new appearances record in his 107th match for England, but he was unable to celebrate a victory. Anastasi gave Italy the lead in the thirty-seventh minute, and Capello (yes, Fabio) made it 2-0 seven minutes after half-time as the England defenders stood waiting for an off-side whistle that never came. It was Italy's first victory against England in nine encounters spread over forty years.

BOBBY: ❛There had been a them-and-us stand-off between the press and the players following some vicious criticism after the defeat in Poland, but they could not have been warmer to me before this game and clubbed together to buy me a wonderful Capo di Monte to mark my record. But the knives were quickly out again after this loose performance against Italy, and I could not help but notice that Alf was being distant after the game.❜

The name conspicuous by its absence from the next two England matches was Bobby Moore. He asked the man to whom he had been a loyal captain for 89 matches if his international career was over. Alf told him: 'I will want you to captain the squad in the World Cup finals.'
    Sadly, it was not a date that England would keep.

Austria, Wembley, 26.9.73. England won 7-0
Shilton   Madeley   Hughes   Bell [1]   McFarland   Hunter
Currie[1]   Channon[2]   Chivers[1]   Clarke[2]   Peters*
Highlights: England over-ran an Austrian defence that had no answer to the combined power of Mike Channon, Martin Chivers and Allan Clarke - the 'top Cs', with Tony

Currie also getting in on the goal spree. It was Currie, Colin Bell and Martin Peters who dictated the pace and pattern of the match from midfield. Channon scored the first goal in the tenth minute, and Clarke struck twice before half-time. Channon and Chivers added goals early in the second-half, and Currie made it 6-0 in the sixty-fourth minute with a rasping shot from the edge of the area. Colin Bell completed the goal avalanche three minutes from the end. 'England can still teach the world how to play,' said Austrian manager Leopold Stastny. But this was a friendly. The test that mattered was to come in the next match. And Bobby Moore was a spectator on the bench.

Poland, Wembley, 17.10.73. Drew 1-1

Shilton Madeley Hughes Bell McFarland Hunter
Currie Channon Chivers (Hector) Clarke[1pen] Peters*

Highlights. England had thirty five goal attempts to two by Poland, but it was the Poles who went through to the World Cup finals at England's expense. Poland had the man of the match in goalkeeper Tomaszewski, who was labelled a clown by Brian Clough. He gave England nothing to laugh about as he saved at least four goals with eccentric but effective goalkeeping. It was Poland who took the lead in the fifty-fifth minute in a rare breakaway raid. Norman Hunter, the most feared tackler in English football, mistimed a challenge out on the touchline and the ball was transferred to unmarked Domarski, whose low shot went under the diving Peter Shilton. Allan Clarke equalised from the penalty spot eight minutes later. England were denied the victory they needed to clinch a place in the World Cup finals when late substitute Kevin Hector headed wide from close range in the last minute of the most frustrating match of Ramsey's reign. It was no consolation that the Poles went on to finish third in the World Cup finals in West Germany the following summer. Anybody who saw this match at Wembley will confirm that it was England who should have gone though if territorial advantage is any measure of a team's superiority. One VIP spectator had no doubt that England deserved to win ...

> *BOBBY:* ❛It was agonising watching from the bench alongside Alf. He completely lost the plot in the second-half when it was obvious we needed to send on a substitute to try to change the pattern of the play. I kept nagging him to make a substitution but his mind seemed to have frozen. By the time he sent on Kevin Hector there were only seconds left. That was the most freakish match ever played at Wembley. If England had won by five or six goals it would have captured their supremacy. Tomaszewski, by a mixture of luck and unorthodox goalkeeping, saved everything that came at him. He was the clown who had the last laugh.❜

CAP 108
Italy, Wembley, 14.11.73. England lost 1-0

Shilton Madeley Hughes Bell McFarland Moore*
Currie Channon Osgood Clarke (Hector) Peters

Highlights. Italy scored their first ever win in England when a certain Fabio Capello netted the only goal of the match in the eighty-seventh minute, steering the ball into the net after Peter Shilton had parried a shot from Chinaglia. England dominated the match for long periods but could not find a way through Italy's superbly organized defence. Veteran Italian playmaker Gianni Rivera was the outstanding player on the pitch, continually slicing open the England defence with a procession of precise passes. We did not know it at the time, but the match marked the hundred and eighth and final appearance of Bobby Moore, arguably the greatest England defender of all time.

BOBBY: ❝Nobody said this was my last international, but I guessed the game was up. I'd had a great run and enjoyed every minute of it, well most of it. It was time for new blood, and while Alf had his sights set on the future I wondered how long before his enemies at the Football Association would bring him down because of things that had happened in the past.❞

The answer was the Spring of 1974. Sir Alf was sacked and given a paper-tissue handshake of £6,500 by a frugal Football Association for whom his World Cup winning team had earned millions. I was then running a PR company in partnership with a well-connected journalist called Peter Lorenzo. We sold Alf's exclusive story to the *Sunday People* for £26,500 and earned him another £7,500 with a British Trade Salutes Sir Alf testimonial dinner at the Café Royal, for which I interviewed Bobby Moore to get background information on all Alf's matches.

It meant I was able to furnish this book with Bobby's views on every match, and gives me the chance to share a true anecdote from the Alf Ramsey testimonial dinner that had Bobby laughing helplessly. The then Prime Minister, Harold Wilson, was the main speaker after the dinner and he sat on the top table between Alf and Bobby.

During the course of his speech a brown mouse ran the length of the table. Its Speedy Gonzales sprint was cut off by recently retired boxing idol Henry Cooper, who caught it in his hammer of a left fist.

Henry handed it to the chef, who in full view of everybody stamped on it. Wilson had no idea this was all going on, and as the audience roared he thought his speech was going down a bomb.

How do you follow that? Only Geoffrey Green could. *The Times* football correspondent, one of the most entertaining after-dinner speakers in the land, was next to pay tribute to Sir Alf. He announced that he would now play the mouse organ. I have often wondered if he released the mouse so that he could use that joke.

He turned to Sir Alf and said: "As you are now out of work, perhaps you would like to join me in a street busking team?"

Geoffrey then produced a harmonica and proceeded to play Moon River. I don't know who was the more surprised and amused, Sir Alf or the PM. It ranks with the funniest after-dinner speeches I have ever heard. Yes, it was Geoffrey in his prime.

Bobby, a master of one-liners, said: "Geoffrey brought the mouse down."

In the autumn of 1966 Bobby and I had shared another memorable 'Top Table' experience. Sir Percy Hoskins, legendary crime investigative reporter for the *Daily Express*, asked me to arrange for Bobby to be guest of honour for the famous Saints and Sinners Club that Percy had set up with bandleader Jack Hylton in 1947. It had 100 specially selected members of the great and the good, ranging from Princes to Prime Ministers and educators to editors. When attending their charity-supporting dinners you had to wear a red carnation if you considered yourself a sinner, and white if you felt you were more a saint.

At the posh Park Lane dinner, Bobby and I – both of us wearing red carnations – sat at the top table either side of conductor/composer Sir Malcolm Sargent of Last Night at the Proms fame. I delivered a short speech outlining Bobby's achievements before he was presented with a silver salver to mark his World Cup captaincy.

Sir Malcolm confided to Bobby and me: "The World Cup final was so dramatic and so exciting that I am planning to set it to music. It will be as compelling as any ballet."

Sadly, within a year Sir Malcolm succumbed to pancreatic cancer and his World Cup Fantasia remained a dream.

Bobby's England career was over, but there were still matches to be played and passes to be made .... and, worryingly, huge debts to be paid.

Chapter 16: Fulham and the Final Final

IT was a rare injury to Bobby that convinced West Ham they could get by without their skipper. He was sidelined for eight weeks with knee ligament problems at the start of 1974, and Mick McGiven did so well in the No 6 shirt that the Hammers decided they could afford to let their most famous player go. The fact that they put a £25,000 fee on his head caused more friction between him and the man to whom he had once been so close, Ron Greenwood.

The previous summer the bright and bombastic Brian Clough had come calling with an audacious £400,000 joint bid for the veteran Moore and the then uncapped Trevor Brooking. He wanted them as a double act in his Derby County team, but the West Ham board turned down the offer.

> *BOBBY*: ❝Cloughie went so far as to take me to dinner at Churchills in London and explained in detail all the things he had in mind for me. He was so convincing, mesmerising even, that he convinced me he would have me winning the League championship and the European Cup under him. 'What I've done for Dave Mackay I can do for you in spades,' he said. I was all ready to sign for him, but Ron Greenwood told me that the board wouldn't agree and that he couldn't sanction the move. He promised me that when the time came for them to let me go it would be without a fee, so that I could negotiate a sort of pension contract for myself. I had a right go at him when he told me six months later that I could go but that the club would want £25,000 for me, even though I had not cost them a penny and after all the service I had given them. It just drove Ron and me further apart.❞

For the record, from 1958 to 1974 Bobby played 642 first-team matches for West Ham, 544 in the First Division and 98 in cup competitions. During that time he won 108 England international caps, eight England Under-23 caps and – earlier – a record 18 England youth caps. He captained England 90 times, equalling the record set in the 1940s and 1950s by Billy Wright.

Norwich manager John Bond, who had been in on the start of the Moore legend at West Ham, tried to sign him, but Bobby was holding out for a hoped-for reunion with another former Hammers clubmate, Malcolm Allison. Then in charge at Crystal

Bobby had his final Final with Fulham against his old club West Ham in 1975

Palace, Big Mal made no secret of his continuing admiration for Moore, but he could not raise the necessary money and so on transfer deadline day, March 14 1974, it was Fulham who landed him with a surprise late offer. Bobby was swayed by the enthusiasm of Fulham skipper Alan Mullery and the often vague but romantic beliefs and ideals of manager Alec Stock, a throwback to the old school who said he qualified as an antique.

In his first full season at Craven Cottage Bobby helped steer Fulham to their first ever FA Cup final. The Great Scriptwriter in the Sky managed to come up with the unlikely scenario that in the opposing dressing-room at Wembley would be West Ham United.

Second Division Fulham were the underdogs, and they went down 2-0 to two goals scored by the virtually unknown Hammers striker Alan Taylor.

EYEWITNESS ALEC STOCK

I had been a member of the Bobby Moore fan club ever since he was a youth team player at West Ham. He oozed class and skill, and played the game in the cultured style I always tried to instill in my teams. When he arrived at Fulham he was into his senior years, and set an example to all the youngsters with his professionalism and totally committed attitude. He and Alan Mullery were the rocks of our team, and helped take us on an adventure that no Fulham supporter will ever forget. We were disappointed by our performance in the final, when two goalkeeping cock-ups cost us dearly, but Bobby played with his usual dignity and elegance. It was a privilege to be able to put his name on my team-sheet, and I was proud to be part of his glorious career.

What only a handful of people knew is that Bobby's move to Fulham coincided with him being buried under a mountain of debt by the collapse of the Woolston Hall Country Club project. He was forced to become a have-boots-will-travel football mercenary, playing for San Antonio Thunder in the United States, and later Seattle Sounders and the Rodney Marsh-managed Carolina Lightnin'. He had the surreal experience in 1976 of captaining Team America against an England X1 in the bicentenary tournament, with Pele among his team-mates.

Playing for Fulham at Blackburn on May 14 1977, Bobby made his 1000th and final first-class appearance. This did not include his performance in the John Huston-directed film *Escape to Victory*, alongside Pele and superstar actors Michael Caine and Sylvester Stallone. One critic claimed that the only thing more wooden than Bobby and some of his footballer colleagues was the goalpost.

His travels later took him to Denmark, South Africa and Hong Kong, where his name stood for everything that was good about the Beautiful Game.

Only in England did it seem he was not wanted. He made a written application for the England manager's job when Don Revie deserted, and did not even get the courtesy of a reply. Elton John gave him the impression he was going to appoint him manager of Watford but instead gave the job to Graham Taylor.

Bobby scratched around in the lower reaches with Oxford City, and persuaded his old chum Harry Redknapp to come back from the United States to join him as assistant manager/coach. Aitch told me: "How could I turn down my hero, the greatest defender that ever breathed. I got on the plane and joined him at Oxford. What a shock I got when I discovered it was not Oxford United in the Football League but Oxford City down in the depths of the Isthmian League. I did not know whether to laugh or cry, but I'd still have come back for Mooro. He was The Master."

Later, Bobby pitched his tent at another struggling club, Southend United before becoming sports editor of the *Sunday Sport*, a paper that peddled soft porn. He then got some dignity back into his life when he became co-commentator to the voluble Jonathan Pearce at Capital Gold. Jonathan has something to shout about now, because he helped restore Bobby's pride when so many had trampled on it.

It screamed out for the Football Association to give him an ambassadorial role, but they blindly and shamefully ignored him.

I had lost contact with Bobby when he went off on his globetrotting adventures, but one day in 1985 I was walking down a back street in Southend when we came face to face, and we hugged like long lost brothers.

In all the years I'd known Bobby I had never seen him looking so radiant. I thought he would be down and depressed because he was out of the major football spotlight, and it was no secret that his marriage had run into trouble.

I was preparing to be sympathetic, but when I asked how he was he responded with glowing sincerity, "Never been better, Norm. Found a lovely lady and have got my life just the way I want it."

We went for a cup of tea together, just like when we'd first met in his apprentice days and I was a young reporter starting out on the journalistic ladder. He told me how proud he was of how his beautiful daughter Roberta and son Dean had turned out, and he then gushed all about the new love of his life, Stephanie Parlane-Moore.

"I'm very lucky," he said, "to have found two wonderful women. Tina was a great wife and mother, but we got married very young before either of us had really lived.

We had a fantastic marriage, then one day six years ago while on a trip to South Africa I was introduced to Stephanie. Sounds corny, but it really was love at first sight. I've had to hurt a lot of people, but I found all I wanted was to be with Steph. Now everything's fine and we've got it all worked out."

As long as I'd been around Bobby, I'd never known him wearing his heart on his sleeve. He usually kept his feelings buried out of sight or smothered by one-line jokes used as a diversionary tactic, but Stephanie had managed to bring the Mills and Boon out of him.

Within a few months of our chance meeting, Tina had divorced him and he had moved into the media world in London and was settled down with the striking and intelligent Stephanie.

John Mitchell, his former Fulham clubmate turned entrepreneur, had opened a new door for him in event management. Only the football doors remained closed to our hero.

The next (and last) time I met him, along with our mutual mate Jimmy Greaves, he had the mark of his terminal illness on him. He was still immaculately dressed but his clothes were hanging on him. Yet we could not help but notice that he was still a very happy man, and it was clearly his new wife Stephanie who had put the spring in his step and the light in his life.

He told us how much he was enjoying his co-commentary work alongside Jonathan Pearce, who was then in his 'shouting fan' phase. "I'm the quiet one," Bobby said.

"Yeah," shot Greavsie, "just like you were when it was your shout at the bar."

He and Greavsie both agreed they would liked to have played with Gazza, who was then the shining new star on the England stage.

"Don't know how Alf would have managed him." said Bobby. "He didn't know how to handle nutters like you, Jimbo."

It was comforting to see Bobby looking so relaxed when it was clear he was seriously ill.

He worked at the microphone right up until virtually the end. His last commentary was on the England 6, San Marino 0 World Cup qualifier at Wembley on February 17 1993. Skipper David Platt scored four goals.

"That's twice as many goals as I scored in all my 108 matches," he told Jonathan, with typical self-effacing humour.

Within a week he had been beaten by his bowel cancer, the silent killer, and the world had lost a good man, Stephanie a loving husband, Roberta and Dean a devoted Dad and football one of its greatest ever defenders. The Master.

TRIBUTES TO THE MASTER

I WAS in Australia when Bobby passed on, trying to sell a television series that was going to be presented by Michael Parkinson. It was called *Who's the Greatest* and one of the proposed episodes would have featured Bobby against Franz Beckenbauer. There was a huge wave of sympathy Down Under when the news broke of Bobby's death, evidence of how his fame as a footballer was world wide.

For the purposes of this tribute section, I contacted as many of his old team-mates and celebrity friends as possible and have also dipped copiously into the tributes that were paid at the time of his passing, several of them from people, like Bobby, sadly no longer with us. We kick off with the two managers who were closest to him:

SIR ALF RAMSEY:

Bobby was my captain, my right hand man, my eyes and ears on and off the pitch. He was the heartbeat of the England team, somebody I could trust with my life. There was not a player who did not look up to him. We would not have won the World Cup if he had not been our skipper. It saddens me so much to have him taken from us at such a young age. For four or more years he was comfortably the best defender in the world.

RON GREENWOOD:

I always hold Bobby up as the example of how the game can and should be played. He was a born leader, and had a bearing that was both dignified and stylish. From the first time I saw him play as a youth international I knew that here was a player who had that indefinable thing called star quality. He had everything: dedication, total commitment, consummate skill and a desire to do everything to perfection. Bobby was a great ambassador for our game. We had our minor differences but never lost respect for each other.

PELE:

There are not words to sum up the grief I feel for the loss of my great friend. We played against each other and together and I know of no finer sportsman or defender. He was a gentleman on and off the pitch, and always played the Beautiful Game in the right spirit. Bobby was a beautiful person and the world is a much poorer place without him. When we exchanged shirts at the end of the 1970 World Cup match it was one of the most moving experiences I ever had on a football pitch. The world of football mourns the loss of one of its greatest ever players.

FRANZ BECKENBAUER:

We were fierce but respectful competitors on the pitch and good friends off it. He was an outstanding captain and I always used him as a barometer of what could be achieved in the game. Whether in victory or defeat, he was sporting and never ever arrogant, and he never gave anything less than his best at all times. There has rarely been a better defensive player in the history of European football. I felt privileged to be on the same pitch, with our exciting World Cup matches most prominent in my memory..

BOBBY CHARLTON:

We have lost one of football's most accomplished players, and the world has lost a thoroughly decent man. He was a magnificent captain who inspired all his team-mates with his high standards and insistence on playing skilfully at all times. While he was a great footballer, I prefer to remember him as a great person. He was a class act. I don't think people realised just what a sharp sense of humour he had. He could be a bit of a rascal with his leg pulling. The way he played the game was the way he was off the pitch, always neat and tidy and with almost an obsession for doing things correctly.

MARTIN PETERS:

Just a few weeks before he died Bobby contacted me about playing in a testimonial match to raise money for Malcolm Allison. That was typical of him, thinking of another before himself. We had some fantastic times together, obviously with the winning of the World Cup in 1966 as the top achievement. He was the best of captains as well as being an outstanding footballer. England were lucky to have him as a leader, because he inspired his team-mates with his 'we're the best' attitude and his wonderful ability both on and off the ball. A man of great character.

GEOFF HURST:

I was honoured to follow Bobby up the Wembley steps three years in succession. He was an exceptional captain and a unique man. Nobody else had Bobby's style and his quiet but steely competitive nature. He *had* to be a winner, but never let his must-win attitude spill over into foul play or bad sportsmanship. We shared some magical times and he became a legend of football. If the World had played Mars the would have been a certainty to be man of the match. The bigger the occasion the better he played.

BOBBY ROBSON:

Bobby followed me into the England team back in 1962 when he was a virtual unknown. My time as an international player was up and I could not have lost my place to a better player. He was majestic, and always carried himself with dignity and style. If ever I am talking to a young footballer about how to conduct himself and the standards to set I always point at Bobby as the perfect example of what can be achieved. It will always puzzle me why he did not make more of an impact on the game after he finished playing. With his experience he had so much to give.

MALCOLM ALLISON:

I cried my eyes out when I realised Bobby had gone. I loved him, not only as a footballer but as a man. From the first time I saw him play at West Ham before he had turned professional I knew that here was somebody with a special talent. Throughout his career he played the game with a poise, a purpose and a pride that put him above the rest. You could find lots of weaknesses in his game, but because of his powers of concentration and his ability to think twice as fast as any defender on earth he always managed to be in the right place at the right time. Football has lost a genius. I have lost a dear, dear friend.

GEORGE BEST:

Bobby was a man apart, a giant of a footballer and a giant of a man. I'm heartbroken that he has been taken from us so young, but he achieved so much as a player that his name will live on as long as football is played. I had the honour and privilege to play with him at Fulham, and we were good mates away from the game. It made no sense that he did not at least get offered a top job in football. He had so much still to give to the game, and could have inspired a whole new generation of footballers. If there has been a better defender born in the UK then I have not seen him. I will miss him desperately

JIMMY TARBUCK:

For a Scouser it is not easy to admit it, but Bobby was the greatest defender I ever saw. Who will every forget his tackle against Jairzinho in the 1970 Word Cup finals against Brazil! That captured in a few seconds what he was all about. He was just unbeatable. I had the pleasure of getting to know Bobby well, and he was as likable – and quietly mischievous – a man as you could meet. He never boasted even though he had much to boast about, and he was the the sort of player and man you could hold up to the kids and say, 'That's the way to do it.'

JOHN LYALL:

I watched Bobby from his earliest days at West Ham, and was in awe at the way he developed into one of the world's greatest defenders. He was a born leader, and gave fantastic service to his club and country. His success did not just happen. He really worked at it and throughout his career was conscientious and dedicated. I remember a game in which the referee was knocked out when the ball hit him in the face. Bobby had the presence of mind to pick up the ref's whistle, blow it to stop the game and summon on the trainer. That was typical of him, always a thought and a deed ahead of everybody else.

RODNEY MARSH:

They should have built statues to Bobby when he was alive, not waited until after he had passed on. We should have let him know how special he was to us, and how highly he was rated. He was by a country mile the greatest defender this country ever produced. We had some great times together at the back end of his career when he was at Fulham. I could not believe it when no major club snapped him up as a manager and I signed him for my then club Carolina Lightnin' as player-coach. It was disgraceful that he was virtually snubbed by the top clubs in England. He was a fantastic footballer, exceptional captain and one of the nicest blokes to cross my path.

KENNY LYNCH:

Bobby and I went back a long way, As well as singing, I was a young footballer in East London when he was starting to make the breakthrough and we became close buddies. We used to hang out together at places like the Ilford Palais before he turned professional at West Ham. He became a magical footballer and all the years I knew him he never once showed off, and liked to be just one of the lads. I was in Mexico for the 1970 World Cup when he showed the world that he was the greatest defender in the tournamentt. I can't believe he's gone. He stood for everything that was best about our football and our country.

PAT JENNINGS

I don't know of any footballer who played with or against Bobby who did not have the utmost respect for him. He was always a fully committed opponent who gave his all in every match, but once the final whistle blew he was a charmer of a man with a quiet but mischievous sense of humour. England were lucky to have such a great defender in their team, and he was a huge reason why they won the World Cup in 1966. It could not have happened to a nicer or more talented man. He was a credit to his country and to professional football. It was an honour to be on the same pitch as him.

HARRY REDKNAPP:

Bobby was sheer class from the top of his head to the tip of his toes, on and off the pitch. There has never been a defender in the British game to match him. He was always perfectly balanced and disciplined, and gave 100 per cent whether he was playing or training. I loved the bloke from my earliest days in the game at West Ham, and had the honour of working with him in Seattle and Oxford. It was so sad that no major club took him on. I'd have taken him on to the staff at Spurs, for sure. He was the neatest person I ever knew. Even when he'd had a lager or three too many he would be completely in control and immaculate in his appearance.

BRIAN CLOUGH:

If I'd had my way Bobby – or Robert as I called him – would have played for me at Derby County. He was a manager's dream, and to have put his name on my team-sheet would have been a privilege. He was a magnificent defender and a composed and iron-willed character, as he proved during that appalling bracelet business in Colombia. If I'd been in charge of the England team I would have led them home in protest. What a way to treat one of our national treasures. Bobby came as close as you can get to the perfect footballer.

EUSEBIO:

Throughout the world Bobby was recognised as one of the greatest defenders ever. He always played in a sporting spirit and never tried to win by foul means. When we played England in the 1966 World Cup semi-final he was exceptional and made it very difficult for me and my Portuguese team-mates to find any space. Nobby Stiles was the player who followed me everywhere like a terrier dog, but when I got past him there was the great Bobby Moore always blocking my way to goal. We met many times socially after that 1966 match and I always found him a real English gentleman.

GORDON BANKS:

It seems like only yesterday that we were following Bobby up the steps at Wembley to collect the World Cup and our medals. I wonder if we would have achieved it without Mr. Cool to lead us. He had such composure and confidence that it could not help but rub off on all the other players. He was all neatness and style in everything that he did, and played without fuss or fear. It was as if he had an in-built radar that told him where to be on the pitch. He always took up the right position and got there before the fastest players in the world, even though he was hardly the quickest thing on two feet. He was a fantastic footballer and a great bloke.

JOHNNY HAYNES:

I was England captain when Bobby made his international debut in 1962. He was still a very young man, but from the moment he pulled on an England shirt it was as if he belonged on the world stage. He was one of the calmest players I ever played with and we used to joke he must have been an eskimo in an earlier life. The mark of a great player is when he seems to have lots of time on the ball while everybody else is scrambling. Bobby seemed to have ages even in a crowded penalty area. He was a Rolls Royce of a player.

KEVIN KEEGAN:

Bobby was every schoolboy's hero when I was just coming into the game, and he set the standards we all tried to meet. His international career was close to ending when mine started, and he went out of his way to make me feel comfortable and relaxed when I joined the England squad. He had a great aura about him, and always played with the composure of a man completely in command of things, You never saw him panic or lose his self control. It was tragic that he went so early, and I could never understand why the FA did not make use of his vast experience and his standing in the game.

FRANK LAMPARD SNR:

I was in awe of Bobby when I started my career at West Ham. He was already established as England captain by the time I made my League debut, but he never came the big I am. He was always encouraging and ready to give advice, and I used to love our after-match sessions at the Black Lion when he would hold court and give an expert analysis of the game. I worked with him at Southend and it was sad to see one of our greatest ever footballers struggling with a minus-nil budget and his team watched by small crowds. He deserved much much better, but never complained. In my eyes he was and always will be a giant.

DENIS LAW:

It was always a battle when I came up against Bobby on the pitch, not so much a physical one as a battle of the minds. He was a fantastic tactical player and you had to have your wits about you to try and get the better of him. You rarely saw him mastered in a match because he was such a good positional player. I looked on him as a great friend away from football and win or lose he was always good company at the bar afterwards. It always amazed me that he did not get a job with one of the top clubs or the Football Association. He had so much still to give to the game. I can't believe he's gone.

RONNIE BOYCE:

I joined West Ham two years after Bobby and saw him growing in stature almost by the minute. He was a commanding and demanding captain but without getting in your face. If you showed discipline and determination he would accept that you were doing your best, but he could be very forceful with his suggestions if you dropped below his standards. He was a quiet man but when he spoke you listened and learned. We all had tremendous respect for him and were lucky to have him as our captain. That was the proudest day of my life when I scored the winner in the 1964 FA Cup final, and I had never known Bobby so visibly happy.

RAY WILSON:

Bobby thrived on responsibility and having a big challenge. He was a baby compared with me because I was six years older, but I wouldn't have wanted the responsibility of captaincy and all the pressures that came with it. But Bobby loved it. He grew at least six inches when Alf made him skipper at 23 and there was no objection from we senior players, because when Alf made a decision it was usually pretty sound. I can never remember him getting in a panic or losing his rag. If we went behind in a match he would step up his game and inspire the rest of us to follow suit. He was not a fist-waving captain but motivated us by the quality of his football. A great man.

NOBBY STILES:

Bobby was born with a footballer's brain. Much of what he did was instinctive and he would take up positions as if on auto pilot. He was only a year older than me, but he gave the impression he was much older, as if he had been here before and done it all. It was this unique manner he had. You just felt at ease with him and yet, in some ways, you didn't know him. He had an aura, someone you could look up to. We were so fortunate to have the best captain in the world. Bobby Moore was not just an outstanding centre-back but also an outstanding person.

WALTER WINTERBOTTOM:

From the first moment I saw Bobby play as a teenage boy I knew that he was going to be a very special player. He had something money cannot buy – poise and presence. While others around him were striving with all their might he seemed to have something to spare and had a maturity that made it seem he was much older than his years. He had he same unique ability as another blond footballer who captained my England team 90 times, Billy Wright. Both became giants of the game and represented their club with dignity and distinction. I knew when I first selected Bobby for England that he would become a permanent fixture. He was made to lead.

DAVID PLATT:

It meant a lot to me that the last match that Bobby watched was the World Cup qualifier in which I was England captain and managed to score four goals against San Marino. I was just six weeks old when Bobby lifted the World Cup in 1966, and I know his legend inside out. His name stands for all that is best about our game. His feats as a defender will live on as long as footballs are kicked. Bobby was a great footballer and great person in every sense, and always had a word of encouragement for young players just starting out. He set the standards we all try to meet. Everywhere I have played in the world people know Bobby Moore. He was the best of British.

BRYAN ROBSON:

When I was growing up Bobby Moore was one of my first heroes, a player whose name was known throughout the world as representative of the way the game could and should be played. He was the greatest of all England captains, and I wanted to emulate him but never could. Just watch film of his performances in the 1966 and 1970 World Cups and you realise that he was a quality player who could organise in the heat of battle and never lose his cool. I would loved to have played with him. The man was sheer class.

GEORGE COHEN:

The gods were smiling down on us when Bobby became our captain. Ray Wilson was the best left-back in the world, and Jack Charlton got everything in the air. But our Bobby was from another planet. He invented ways of defending, perfecting his positional play to compensate for his lack of pace. He was just simply special. Bobby almost invented the sweeper role, and was always perfectly balanced when making a tackle. You rarely saw him off his feet There were few defenders who could match him for making a positive and accurate pass out of defence. He was continually looking to launch counter attacks. On top of all that he was a lovely bloke.

FRANK McLINTOCK:

I could not believe it when Bobby was taken from us so early. When it became clear how seriously ill he was I just could not hold back the tears. He had been my opponent on the pitch and my good friend off it. Bobby was one of the best footballers I have ever seen. He dwarfed most other players with his consistent brilliance. At all times he was calm in a crisis and brought order when all around him was mayhem. We Scots knew how lucky England were to have such an exceptional footballer leading them into the 1966 World Cup, and he proved in the 1970 tournament that he was clearly the best defender in the world. Did you see his tackle against Jairzinho? Enough said.

NOEL CANTWELL:

My heart has been broken by the passing of my friend, who I knew from the opening days of his football career. I was best man at his first wedding but he was always the best man on the football field. They said he couldn't run, but he was rarely beaten to the ball. They said that he couldn't jump, but he was rarely beaten in the air. He recognised his weaknesses and compensated by working hard on the training pitch and focusing on his positional play. He was a footballing master, and a lovely, lovely gentle man. If anybody ever asks me who was the greatest defender I ever saw I have no hesitation in saying Bobby Moore.

THE BOBBY MOORE TIMELINE

Robert Frederick Chelsea Moore (Chelsea is a family name, and nothing to do with the Stamford Bridge club)

1941, April 12: Born Upney Hospital, Barking, during a Luftwaffe blitz.

Parents: Robert (Bob), a gasfitter and electrician. Mother Doris (Doss).

Schools: Westbury Primary, Barking, 1946 to 1952, then Tom Hood Technical High School in Leyton from 1952 to 1957. Gets 8 O-levels in his last year at school.

1956: Signs amateur forms for West Ham United. Makes debut for West Ham colts on October 6 1956.

1957, October 2: England Youth team debut in Holland, won 3-2.

1957, December 2: Debut for West Ham reserves.

1957: Captains England in Euro Youth Championships (Runners-Up)

1958: Signs Professional forms for West Ham.

1958, September 8: Debut for West Ham first-team in a 3-2 win over Manchester United at Upton Park. West Ham: Gregory; Bond, Cantwell; Malcolm, Brown, Moore; Grice, Smith, Keeble, Dick, Musgrove.

1960, November 2: Debut England Under 23s, 1-1 v Italy at Newcastle

1961, November 5: Sent off for a retaliatory kick at Manchester City winger David Wagstaffe in the last minute of a First Division match at Maine Road.

1962, April 20: Captains West Ham for the first time v. Cardiff City.

1962, May 20: England debut v. Peru in Lima, win 4-1. Takes Bobby Robson's place for the four matches in the 1962 World Cup finals in Chile. Lose 3-1 to eventual champions Brazil in the quarter-finals.

1962, June 30: Marries Elizabeth (Tina) Dean at St Clement's Church, Ilford. West Ham skipper Noel Cantwell is best man just before signing for Manchester United. Honeymoons in Majorca.

1963, May 20: Captains England for the first time v Czechoslovakia in Prague. His 12th cap, and leads the team to a 4-2 victory.

1964, May: Elected Footballer of the Year by the Football Writers' Association.

1964, May 2 1964: Collects FA Cup as West Ham captain after a 3-2 victory over Preston in the final at Wembley.

1964, November: Has a cancerous testicle surgically removed in a secret operation.

1965, January 1965: Daughter Roberta born.

1965, May 19: Collects European Cup Winners Cup after a 2-0 victory over TSV Munich 1860 in the final at Wembley.

1966, July 1: Signs new contract with West Ham so that he is eligible to play for England in the World Cup.

1966, July 30: Collects the Jules Rimet trophy after captaining England to a 4-2 victory over West Germany in the World Cup final at Wembley. Makes a perfect pass to open the way for Geoff Hurst to complete an historic hat-trick.

1966: Elected BBC Sports Personality of the Year and *Daily Express* and Sports Writers' Association Sportsman of the Year.

1967: Awarded an OBE in the New Year's Honours list.

1968, March 24: Son Dean born.

1968, June 8: Captains England to third place in the Euro championships. Beat Russia 2-0 in the play-off in Rome after losing 1-0 to Yugoslavia in the semo-final.

1969: Captains England on a summer tour during which they draw 0-0 with Mexico, beat Uruguay 2-1 and lose 2-1 to Brazil in Rio.

1970, May 26: Arrested on a trumped-up jewel theft charge in Bogota.

1970, June: Captains England in World Cup, including a classic match with eventual champions Brazil. They go out to West Germany in quarter-finals after leading 2-0.

1970, July: A kidnap threat is reported against Bobby's children and a £10,000 ransom demanded. The Moore household is put under surveillance. Shortly afterwards the police get a tip-off that Bobby is going to be shot during a match. Neither threat comes to anything and nobody is ever charged. Comedian Bobby says: "Can't Ron just drop me rather than have me shot?"

1971, January 5: Suspended for two weeks and fined £200 by West Ham for drinking at a Blackpool nightclub on the eve of a Cup tie against Blackpool that West Ham lost 4-0 on a skating rink of a surface. Sir Alf Ramsey omits him from the team for a European championship match against Malta in Valletta.

1972, February 14: Wins 100th Cap v. Scotland at Hampden Park, England power to a 5-0 victory on a snow-carpeted pitch.

1973, February 17: Overtakes Jimmy Ruffell's West Ham appearance record with his 509th club game.

1973, July: West Ham turn down a £400,000 joint transfer offer from Derby County for Bobby and Trevor Brooking.

1973, November 14: Plays his 108th and final game for England against Italy at Wembley.

1974, January 5 1973: Damages knee ligaments in what is his last ever first-team game for West Ham against Hereford in an FA Cup tie.

1974, March 9: Final game in a West Ham shirt in a reserve match against Plymouth Argyle.

1974, March 14: Joins Fulham on transfer deadline day for a £25,000 fee. Norwich City manager John Bond had made an earlier bid.

1974, March 19: Fulham debut at Craven Cottage. Fulham lose 4-0 to Middlesborough.

1975, May 3: Collects FA Cup runners-up medal with Fulham at Wembley. West Ham are the 2-0 winners.

1976: Joins San Antonio Thunder for the summer season.

1976, May 31: Captains Team America, including Pele, in a bicentennial international against England. Lose 3-1.

1976, October 10: Fulham team threaten to walk off in protest after Bobby is red carded for showing dissent in a League Cup tie at Bolton.

1977, May 14 1977: Final game for Fulham v. Blackburn Rovers. It is Bobby's 1000th first-class game.

1978: Joins the Harry Redknapp-coached Seattle Sounders.

Artist Art Turner captures the final handshake with Ron Greenwood on the day Bobby left West Ham for Fulham

Art Turner

1979: Player-coach for six months of Danish 3rd Division club Herning.

1979-1981: Manager of Oxford City, with Harry Redknapp as his No 2.

1983: Coaches Team Eastern Athletic in Hong Kong.

1984-86: Chief executive and then manager of Southend United.

1986, January 6: Tina Moore divorces him. Bobby had already set up home with Stephanie-Parlane Moore, a senior air stewardess he had first met in 1979 t

1986: Becomes sports editor of the down-market tabloid, *Sunday Sport.* He has a 'heart attack' scare and is rushed to hospital, but it is diagnosed as as hyperventilation.

1990: Joins Capital Gold Radio as football analyst and co-commentator to Jonathan Pearce. Sets up Mitchell-Moore Associates with ex-Fulham team-mate John Mitchell

1991, April 22: Operation for Cancer of the colon.

1991, December 4: Marries his long-time partner Stephanie Parlane-Moore at Chelsea register office.

1993, February 15: Releases public statement about his illness.

1993, February 17: Makes his final appearance at Wembley Stadium, co-commentating with Jonathan Pearce on the England 6, San Marino 0 World Cup qualifier.

1993, February 24: Bobby passes away in Wansdsworth, aged 51.

1993, March 2: Funeral at Putney Vale Crematorium. His ashes are buried in a plot with those of his parents

1993, March 6: Geoff Hurst and Martin Peters place a giant floral No 6 shirt in claret and blue colours on the centre-circle before the home League game against Wolves, and the club announces that Bobby's old No 6 shirt will be 'rested'.

1993, June 28: A memorial service is held at Westminster Abbey, with Franz Beckenbauer, Michael Parkinson, Bobby Charlton, Kenneth Wolstenhome and Jimmy Tarbuck among those who make tribute contributions.,

2003: Bobby Moore statue unveiled by Prince Andrew at Green Street, Upton Park,

2007: Sir Bobby Charlton unveils an 18 foot statue at Wembley.

THE GAMES BOBBY PLAYED

England Caps: 108, 90 as Captain. Only Peter Shilton (125) and David Beckham (115) have played more times for England. Bobby shares with Billy Wright (105 caps, 1946-59) the record of captaining England 100 times. Under 23 Caps: 8. England Youth Caps: 18

Bobby scored just two goals for England in his 108 matches, both in the World Cup year of 1966 – in the 1-1 draw with Poland at Anfield and then in the 6-1 thrashing of Norway in Oslo a month before the World Cup triumph over West Germany at Wembley.

West Ham Appearances: Football League games 544; FA Cup ties 36; League Cup ties 49. European ties: 13. Total: 642. Goals 27 (25 League, 3 League Cup)

Fulham Appearances: Football League games 124; FA Cup ties 15; League Cup -ties 11. Total: 150. 1 goal.

Honours:

World Cup winners' medal 1966

European championship bronze medal 1968

European Cup Winners' Cup 1965

FA Cup winners medal 1964 (West Ham)

FA Cup runners-up medal 1975 (Fulham)

League Cup runners-up 1966

World Cup Player of Players 1966

Football Writers' Footballer of the Year 1964; *Daily Express* Sportsman of the Year 1966; Sports Writers' Association Sportsman of the Year 1966 (collected on behalf of the team),

European Footballer of the Year, runner-up to Gerd Muller 1970; Hammer of the Year 1961, 1963, 1968, 1970.

Awarded OBE 1967.

A magnificent 18ft high statue of Bobby stands tall and proud at his second home of Wembley, stunningly crafted by sculptor Phillip Jackson. It was unveiled in 2007 by his England team-mate Sir Bobby Charlton.

On the plinth are perfectly chosen words composed by our mutual friend Jeff Powell of the Daily Mail:

"Immaculate footballer, Imperial defender, Immortal hero of 1966, First Englishman to raise the World Cup aloft, National treasure, Master of Wembley, Lord of the game, Captain extraordinary, Gentleman for all time."

Other Books By Norman Giller

www.normangillerbooks.com

Banks of England (with Gordon Banks) **Footballing Fifties** **The Lane of Dreams**
The Glory and the Grief (with George Graham) **Banks v Pelé** (with Terry Baker)
Football And All That (A history of the Beautiful Game) **Seventies Revisited** (with Kevin Keegan)
The Final Score (with Brian Moore) **ABC of Soccer Sense** (with Tommy Docherty)
The Glory Glory Game (SWC) **Billy Wright, A Hero for All Seasons** (official biography)
The Rat Race (with Tommy Docherty) **Denis Compton** (The Untold Stories)
McFootball, the Scottish Heroes of the English Game **The Golden Double** (with Terry Baker)
The Book of Rugby Lists (with Gareth Edwards) **The Book of Tennis Lists** (with John Newcombe)
Chopper's Chelsea (with Ron Harris) **Hammers80** (introduced by Sir Trevor Brooking)
World Cup 2010 Day By Day *Satzenbrau* **Sports Puzzle Book** *Satzenbrau* **TV Puzzle Book**
The Book of Golf Lists **TV Quiz Trivia** **Sports Quiz Trivia**
Know What I Mean (with Frank Bruno) **Eye of the Tiger** (with Frank Bruno)
From Zero to Hero (with Frank Bruno) **The Judge Book of Sports Answers**
My Most Memorable Fights (with Henry Cooper) **How to Box** (with Henry Cooper)
Henry Cooper's 100 Greatest Boxers **Sir Henry Cooper** A Hero for All Time (2012)
Mike Tyson Biography **Mike Tyson, the Release of Power** (with Reg Gutteridge)
Crown of Thorns, the World Heavyweight Championship (with Neil Duncanson)
Fighting for Peace (Barry McGuigan biography, with Peter Batt)
World's Greatest Cricket Matches **World's Greatest Football Matches**
Golden Heroes (withDennis Signy) **Watt's My Name** (with Jim Watt)
The Judge (1,001 arguments settled) **The Great Football IQ Quiz Book** (The Judge of *The Sun*)
The Marathon Kings **The Golden Milers** (with Sir Roger Bannister)
Olympic Heroes (with Brendan Foster) **Olympics Handbook 1980** **Olympics Handbook 1984**
Book of Cricket Lists (Tom Graveney) **Top Ten Cricket Book** (Tom Graveney)
Cricket Heroes (Eric Morecambe, for Lord's Taverners) **Big Fight Quiz Book** **TVIQ Puzzle Book**
Lucky the Fox (with Barbara Wright) **Gloria Hunniford's TV Challenge**
The Contenders (novel) **The Concorde Club** The First 50 Years (with Cole Mathieson)
Comedy novels: **Carry On Doctor Carry On England Carry On Loving**
Carry On Up the Khyber Carry On Abroad Carry On Henry What A Carry On
A Stolen Life e-novel) **Mike Baldwin: Mr Heartbreak** (novel) **Hitler's Final Victim** (e-novel)
The Glory and the Greed (e-novel)
Books in collaboration with **RICKY TOMLINSON**
Football My Arse Celebrities My Arse Cheers My Arse Reading My Arse (The Rock Island Line)
PLUS books in collaboration with **JIMMY GREAVES**:
This One's On Me **This One's On Me Revisited**
The Final (novel) **The Ball Game** (novel) **The Boss** (novel)
The Second Half (novel) **Let's Be Honest** (with Reg Gutteridge) **Greavsie's Heroes and Entertainers**
World Cup History GOALS! **Stop the Game, I Want to Get On**
The Book of Football Lists Taking Sides Funny Old Games (with The Saint)
Sports Quiz Challenge Sports Quiz Challenge 2
It's A Funny Old Life Saint & Greavsie's 1990 World Cup Special
The Sixties Revisited Don't Shoot the Manager
Jimmy Greaves At 70 (with Terry Baker and Michael Giller)